Managing Information Technology

Recent Titles in
The Libraries Unlimited Library Management Collection
Formerly entitled Greenwood Library Management Collection

Creating the Agile Library: A Management Guide for Librarians
Lorraine J. Haricombe and T. J. Lusher, editors

Young Adults and Public Libraries: A Handbook of Materials and Services
Mary Anne Nichols and C. Allen Nichols, editors

Moving Library Collections: A Management Handbook
Elizabeth Chamberlain Habich

Leadership and Academic Librarians
Terrence F. Mech and Gerard B. McCabe, editors

Planning for a New Generation of Public Library Buildings
Gerard B. McCabe

Leadership and Administration of Successful Archival Programs
Bruce W. Dearstyne, editor

Video Collection Development in Multi-type Libraries: A Handbook, Second
Edition
Gary Handman, editor

Expectations of Librarians in the 21st Century
Karl Bridges, editor

The Modern Public Library Building
Gerard B. McCabe and James R. Kennedy, editors

Human Resource Management in Today's Academic Library: Meeting
Challenges and Creating Opportunities
Janice Simmons-Welburn and Beth McNeil, editors

Exemplary Public Libraries: Lessons in Leadership, Management and Service
Joy M. Greiner

Managing Information Technology

A Handbook for Systems Librarians

Patricia Ingersoll

Associate Director and Associate Professor
Penrose Library, University of Denver

and

John Culshaw

Associate Professor and Faculty Director for Systems
University of Colorado at Boulder

Libraries Unlimited Library Management Collection
Gerard B. McCabe, Series Adviser

LIBRARIES
U N L I M I T E D
A Member of the Greenwood Publishing Group

Westport, Connecticut • London

Library of Congress Cataloging-in-Publication Data

Ingersoll, Patricia.
   Managing information technology : a handbook for systems librarians /
Patricia Ingersoll and John Culshaw.
     p. cm. – (Libraries Unlimited library management collection, ISSN 0894-2986)
   Includes bibliographical references and index.
   ISBN 0-313-32476-X (alk. paper)
   1. Academic libraries—Automation—Management. 2. Systems librarians—Handbooks,
manuals, etc. 3. Academic libraries—Administration—Handbooks, manuals, etc. 4.
Academic libraries—Technological innovations. I. Culshaw, John, 1964- II. Title. III.
Series.
Z675.U5I574 2004
025.1'977—dc22   2004048638

British Library Cataloguing in Publication Data is available.

Library of Congress Catalog Card Number: 2004048638
ISBN: 0-313-32476-X
ISSN: 0894-2986

First published in 2004

Libraries Unlimited, 88 Post Road West, Westport, CT 06881
A Member of the Greenwood Publishing Group, Inc.
www.lu.com

Printed in the United States of America

The paper used in this book complies with the
Permanent Paper Standard issued by the National
Information Standards Organization (Z39.48–1984).

10 9 8 7 6 5 4 3 2 1

"Checklist for Testing New Software" by Donald A. Barclay was reprinted from *Managing Public Access Computers: A How-To-Do-It Manual for Librarians* with permission of the publishers. Copyright © 2000 by Neal-Schuman Publishers Inc.

All URLs cited in the text were retrieved in February 2004.

Contents

List of Illustrations. ix
Acknowledgments. xi
Introduction and Rationale xiii
    Some Historical Notes. ix

1—Planning 1
    Strategic Planning. 3
    Policy Development 4
    Budget. 7
    Planning Tools 7
    Writing a Technology Plan. 10
    Project Management. 10
    Statistics and Decision Making. 11
    Integrated Library System Migration 13
    Local Standards 17
    Replacement Cycles 18
    Disaster Preparedness and Recovery 20

2—Staffing and Reporting Lines 23
    The Systems Librarian 25
    Teams and Hierarchies 28
    Organization Charts 29
    Centralization and Branches. 30
    Telecommuting. 33
    Recruiting 34
    Job Descriptions and Performance Reviews. 36

3—Communication 39
    Collegiality 41
    Supporting Library Patrons. 42
    Professional Reading 43
    Research and Scholarship. 44
    Leadership. 45
    Stress. 46

4—Interorganizational Relationships 49
Stakeholders 49
National Organizations 50
Vendors 51

5—Development 55
Technology Fees 56
Grants 57

6—Service and Support 59
Service Orientation 60
Help Desk Services 61
Service Standards and Measures 64

7—Training 67
Training Approaches 68
Campus Resources 69
Professional Organizations and User Groups 70
Professional Education 70
Staff Development and Continuing Education 73

8—Daily and Periodic Operations 77
Prototype, Test, Configure, and Deploy 79
Hardware Maintenance 81
Printing Issues 83
CD-ROM and DVD 84
Software Upgrades and Monitoring 86
License Control 87
Server Management 89
Data Protection and Backups 91
Security 92
Departmental Procedures 95
Logs and Record Keeping 96
Inventory 96
Statistical Reports and Analyses 97
Programming 98
Link Checking 99

9—Space 101
Facilities 101
Infrastructure 103
LAN, Phone, and Other Cabling 105
Wireless Computing 106
Ergonomics and Safety 107

10—Research and New Technologies. 109
Teaching and Learning in a Web-based World 111
Mission-Critical Technologies 111
Evaluation of New Technologies 112
Impacts and Applications of International Standards. 112
Portals. 115
Digital Library Initiatives 116
Mobile Computing 120
Web Logs 122
Videoconferencing 123
Interactive Chat. 124
Intranets 125
Document Delivery. 125

11—Summary 127
Trends in Technology. 128
Trends in Higher Education 130

Resource Materials 133
Account Policy 134
Example of a LAN Account Policy 134
Appropriate Use Policy. 135
Automation Consultants 137
Business Continuity Plan Questionnaire. 138
Computer Census Form 149
Example of a Pre-Installation Worksheet. 149
Cleaning Up Your Hard Drive 149
Computer Equipment Replacement Plan 151
Controlled Circulation Publication List 154
Decision-making Model 155
ILS Vendor Information 157
Job Description Form 158
Job Evaluation Form. 159
Library Technology Plan 164
I. Electronic Content Acquisition 164
II. Electronic Content Creation. 165
III. Shared IT Infrastructure Services 167
IV. Scholarly Collaboration 172
Appendices 172
Online Help Page 173
Password Policy and Instructions. 174
Professional Reading 175
Selected Acronyms. 176
Server Configuration Reference Sheet 178
Supported Software Policy. 179

Web Site URLs. 180

References. 183
Additional Reading. 191

Index. 193

List of Illustrations

Figure 1.1. Cost-effectiveness. 9

Figure 1.2. Computer rotation budget. 19

Figure 2.1. Organizational tree chart 31

Figure 2.2. Chart based on system theory. 32

Figure 2.3. Team-based chart 33

Figure 8.1. Open systems interconnection (OSI) reference model. 78

Figure 10.1. Checklist for testing new software. 113

Acknowledgments

We are grateful to Nancy Allen and Jennifer Kutzik for reviewing our manuscript prior to publication. We could not have undertaken a project like this without the generous support of the libraries in which we have worked and our numerous mentors and colleagues too numerous to mention.

Special thanks to the Systems Departments at the University of Colorado at Boulder and the University of Denver for their patience while we completed this project.

Introduction and Rationale

Information technology permeates practically every element of library service, but librarians often find themselves ill prepared to manage the ever-increasing number of electronic information delivery systems. Many librarians completed their graduate degree before technology pervaded libraries. Perhaps library school imparted a theoretical framework but overlooked the pragmatics of day-to-day operations in a busy systems office. Some librarians eventually discover that they possess the instincts to resolve a technical crisis like a printer jam or software installation. Librarians who are willing to experiment with technology or read instruction manuals will be sought out for advice and may one day find that they are recognized as systems librarians. The metamorphosis and staffing of a systems office is an ongoing phenomenon, but this book attempts to offer guidance to anyone suddenly elevated to this challenging position. Responsibilities vary from library to library of course, but the appointment of a systems librarian is the norm.

For current purposes, *information technology* is the term used to designate the broad field encompassing areas such as telecommunications and networking, information delivery, office systems, expert systems, digitization, speech recognition, hardware and software, data formats, and database systems. The "systems department" is generally responsible for the library's information technology infrastructure and services. Many excellent historical overviews document how technology has changed libraries and how the discipline of systems librarianship has evolved. This volume offers only a brief historical background sketch; it begins from the present to help systems librarians better plan for tomorrow.

This volume reflects the experience of thirty years of learning on-the-job in academic libraries. Our advisors maintain that, with a little imagination, the guidance offered here applies in other kinds of library environments as well. We consider both the roles and services of the information technology organization. The chapters titled "Planning," "Staffing, and Reporting Lines," "Communication," "Interorganizational Relationships," and "Development" consider some of the more theoretical roles of the information technology manager. Subsequent chapters, including "Service and Support," "Training," "Daily and Periodic Operations," "Space," and "Research and New Technologies," shift to a more applied discussion of services provided. The text provides introductory material on a range of topical areas, practical tools, tips, and advice. Supplemental resources are provided when appropriate. Appended resource materials provide a glossary; sample job descriptions; organizational charts; integrated library system vendor contacts; suggested professional reading; controlled circulation publications; a bibliography, sample policies, and documents; and an index.

Some Historical Notes

Before looking at the roles and services typically performed by today's systems librarians, it is interesting to take a brief look at the profession's beginnings and history. In many ways, the discipline of systems librarianship was born of skepticism. IBM and other companies started working with libraries in the 1950s. These early efforts were primarily focused on circulation control. Librarians were uncertain of the effects of automation. Would only large libraries be affected? Or was automation too expensive so only small libraries would benefit (Jones, 1956)? Throughout the 1950s and 1960s, libraries continued to study new technologies and were hesitantly integrating them into workflow and services. Nevertheless, Wasserman (1965) explained that there was an odd dichotomy at work in American libraries. Most librarians were personally terrified of the computer, but the profession as a whole maintained a keen interest in new technologies. The Library of Congress put significant effort into the development of the MARC (Machine Readable Cataloging) standard in the 1960s. Beyond MARC, the Library was also working with other research libraries, foundations, and businesses to push the progress of developing automation for libraries.

By the 1970s, some of the uncertainties of the previous decades were starting to fade, and it was becoming clear that automation would have a huge impact on library operations and services. For example, the series *Advances in Librarianship* began publication in 1970 with the goal of providing scholarly reviews summarizing significant current professional topics. The lead article in the premier volume was Piternick's "The Machine and Cataloging." F. W. Lancaster published his pivotal *Toward Paperless Information Systems* in 1978. The impact of that work in libraries set the stage for the information technology explosion of the 1980s. OCLC, founded as the Ohio College Library Center in 1967, became available to libraries nationwide in 1977. The stability of the MARC cataloging format led many libraries to create or purchase online integrated library systems in the 1980s.

By the late 1980s, the academic library was encountering rapid change. Sapp and Gilmour (2002) indicate that "new roles were emerging and traditional ones were evolving, blurring, and in some cases disappearing" (p. 571). Personal computers and CD-ROM technology quickly increased the presence of technology in academic libraries of the 1980s and 1990s. Libraries without integrated management systems were investing in them. Those with first generation systems were migrating to new systems. The Internet and the World Wide Web cemented the place of technology in libraries and perhaps within society as a whole.

The first systems librarians were dubbed data-processing experts. Several large libraries had individuals assigned to systems librarian-like roles in the 1960s. There was even a debate in the professional literature over the best preparation for this so-called new breed of librarians. Should systems librarians be trained in librarianship and then specialize in technology? Or should the library seek technologists to work in the library (Wasserman, 1965)? This is a question that some libraries still debate today. Wasserman called data-processing experts the "modern hero of librarianship." In many ways, that characterization of systems librarians has not changed as the profession studies and implements cutting-edge technologies.

As automation took hold in academic librarians, the position of systems librarian became the norm rather than the exception. For many years, systems librarians were part of the library's technical services operation. Martin (1988) theorized that this was simply a "holdover from the early days of library automation" (p. 60). As time went on, individuals in these positions came from a variety of backgrounds. For example, when Virginia Tech established its Automation Services Department in 1986, the first professional to fill that position had sixteen years of public services and collection management experience at two universities (Kriz & Queijo, 1989). Tom Wilson was coordinator of mediated searching at the University of Houston Libraries before becoming a systems librarian (Wilson, 1989, 1998). Individuals with computer science degrees can make more money in the private sector, so systems librarianship has evolved as a profession with a variety of career paths (Laurence, 1997). Still others "accidentally" happened upon systems librarianship as described by Rachel Singer Gordon. In her *Accidental Systems Librarian,* Gordon (2003) explains that she became a systems librarian because she "liked computers and was comfortable with some of the basics" (p. 24).

According to Lavagnino (1997), there have been four stages in the evolution of the systems librarian. Artifacts of the first stage were typewriters and adding machines. Manifested in the second stage were mainframe and minicomputers, function-specific automated systems, emphasis on automating technical tasks, offline batch processing, and online timesharing systems. The third stage brought integrated online systems, online public access catalogs (OPACs), and microcomputers. Harbingers of the latest stage include the preeminence of networking, a focus on Transmission Control Protocol/Internet Protocol (TCP/IP) applications, accelerated standards development and adoption, servers replacing mainframes and minicomputers, and a distributed client/server environment. The latest stage changed the nature of what systems librarians do. There is an increase in the direct support of patrons. Campus computing centers became colleagues instead of service providers. Collaborative activities increased both among colleagues in the library as well as with external partners such as vendors, consortia, and other libraries. Systems librarians became more knowledgeable in external hardware, software, and networking. Commitments to administrative and professional tasks grew, as did systems office staffing. A systems librarian had to become more of a generalist in focus. Reporting lines shifted, with systems librarians reporting to the library director. The systems librarian position has gradually become a key role in most library organizational charts.

Only one systems librarian position was advertised in *American Libraries* in 1974, but the number of advertised positions had increased to 43 by 1994 (Lavagnino, 1997). As the pace of technological change accelerates, the number of librarians specializing in systems will increase proportionately. Digital initiatives, new technologies, and the need for steady, reliable service are beginning to show that larger organizations require more than one systems specialist.

Several authors have studied the history of systems librarianship and its impact on academic libraries in more detail than the scope of this book. See the section titled "A Brief History of Computing in Libraries" in *The Systems Librarian* (Wilson, 1998). Michael Gorman's (1987) article, "Organization of Academic Libraries in the Light of Automation," puts systems work into perspective in the time period just before the Internet had its impact on libraries. Finally, although not solely focused on systems librarianship, Sapp and Gilmour's (2002) article on the history of academic libraries does offer an interesting examination of the discipline. This article is especially useful in terms of systems librarianship because of the authors' use of citation-tracking of the work of F. W. Lancaster in their research.

Planning

Change is a central element in the growth of any organization. Today, the accelerating rate of change in the technology arena is frequently the driving force for change at every level of the organization. "The forces promoting stability without introducing change in an organization (i.e., stagnation) are both pervasive and powerful" (Quinlan, 1991, p. 86). Change can precipitate anxiety and resistance within organizations that are often difficult to overcome. Careful and thorough planning is essential to successful implementation in any project and helps overcome resistance to change. Change represents a strategy to achieve goals, not an end in itself. Targeted goals should represent the shared values of the organization and be clearly stated as such. Some shared values within libraries are easily identifiable; some require a process of identification.

Libraries in the twenty-first century need to balance the strong external forces of change with the resistance to change. Such resistance is a common trait of many longtime library workers who might desire to do things as they have always been done. This balance is essential to encourage ongoing development of services and collections in an age of rapid technological change. Beyond being essential, this is a challenge as well, because many library services and policies are based on years of tradition as paper-based organizations. As users grow their information literacy skills and increase their reliance on the Internet as a research tool, libraries must constantly evolve and employ new technologies so as not to become irrelevant.

Balanced planning involves an ability to make choices and decisions within a limited resource pool. Over time, the results of planning may appear to be a straight line between Point A and Point B, but every point along the line itself represents a decision—a "Yes" and a "No." In other words, every decision in the course of forward progress means learning to say *yes* to some ideas and *no* to others. Learning to say no is not necessarily the path to popularity, but all managers must learn to accept occasional personal unpopularity to further the goals of the organization. Good managers must learn the difference between possibility and feasibility; they must learn to say no some of the time.

Boss (1997) defines the essential ingredients of planning as "problem definition, analysis, synthesis, evaluation, and iteration" (p. 148). Not every project lends itself to a formal planning process, but there are more informal options available. The focus of research and planning, especially technology planning, has shifted through time. Technology planning has become more central to all planning as technology has become more pervasive in every aspect of people's work. Hatcher (1995) notes that "larger libraries find a need for more planning and management and less day-to-day operational work from their systems librarians" (p. 107). This means that the systems librarian is no longer fixing printers or installing memory in computers. Instead, the systems librarian is likely to supervise a staff of information technology (IT) professionals. The IT staff, in effect, becomes the front line, and the systems librarian assumes a managerial role facilitating planning, budgets, and future directions.

Historically, the acquisition of an automated system, its functionality, and improving the human–machine interface were key goals of the systems office. As technologies mature, the focus of planning shifts. The integrated library system is now just one element of the library's technological infrastructure. The systems office must also support other systems, like portal products or specific productivity tools (such as Clio for interlibrary loan support, relational database software such as MySQL for management of project-related metadata, or ColdFusion for Web development). Planning does not occur in a vacuum. The systems librarian will often be involved in planning activities at the campus or university level. This can include planning for campuswide policies or services in which the library is a key partner or agent, such as a pay-for-print or student portal initiatives. Currently, there is increasing examination of the impact of technology on planning and how it dominates planning discussions. Personnel data in an electronic format, for example, can be incorporated into the entire planning process without recreating each report separately. This is one example of a data interdependency that makes up part of the overall planning perspective. The systems librarian plays an important role in helping colleagues decide how technology can best be utilized to support future projects.

Each of the eleven sections in this chapter addresses specific planning issues encountered by the typical systems office. Section topics include a discussion of strategic planning, policy development, planning tools available, writing a technology plan, project management, statistics and decision making, integrated library system (ILS) migration, standards, budget, rotation planning, and disaster preparedness and recovery.

Strategic Planning

Briefly, strategic planning entails the endorsement of a mission statement and the enumeration of the related goals and objectives that support it. The mission and goals should reflect those principles that the organization values highly. Strategic planning should result in tactical planning, and tactical planning should result in action. Action produces outcomes to reevaluate and feed back into revisions of the plan. In some cases, consultants can be useful in the strategic planning process, but there are convincing arguments against this course of action. A good consultant facilitates discussions with impartiality; White (1990) cautions, however, that some consultants may be sound in theory but lacking in practical library experience. Discuss whether a consultant is the best option for your situation. If the library decides to proceed with a consultant, spend time selecting the best consultant for your environment. Strategic planning without an outside consultant can still be effective. If the library pursues this activity utilizing internal staff, select an individual or group of individuals with the abilities and personalities to foster long-term planning efforts by encouraging all colleagues to embrace the future vision and outcome of the process.

At the outset, the library will need to determine whether the planning exercise is broad in focus (i.e., addresses all areas of the library) or narrow (i.e., examines a specific topic such as information technology). Some libraries and many universities have developed strategic plans that focus on information technology. Others have created strategic plans that are broader in scope and identify how technology supports all aspects of the plan. The type of planning you undertake will depend on your environment and the expected outcomes.

There have been lively debates about whether there is a future for libraries, or whether they may face extinction. Strategic planning is one way to visualize what the library will look like in the future and plan specific ways to attain the ideal scenario in three years, five years, or some other time interval. It is difficult to predict the actual technologies that will be employed in the future, so strong direction and vision are vital outcomes of a strategic planning process. "To avoid stagnation, all organizations need to think strategically about what they are doing and why. The strategic management of change requires living in an anticipatory state, keeping attuned to internal and external environmental factors and recognizing that lack of change augers an unappealing or nonexistent future" (Quinlan, 1991, p. 87). Library leaders believe libraries can remain viable if they position themselves to become "a hybrid institution that contains both digital and book collections" (*Buildings, Books, and Bytes*, 1996). Future libraries are not just about collections but about services and facilities that support the changing needs of its clientele. These also need to be addressed to create a relevant strategic plan.

Planning can help the library understand its relationship and scope of services within the context of its various external constituencies. Identifying environmental factors will lead planners to examine the needs of the university and its current programs, overall trends in higher education, as well as trends in technology. The central focus of planning is on the needs of library users because that is the most commonly shared value of libraries. The relationship between libraries and users operates bilaterally. One of the findings of a 1996 study by the Benton Foundation, which employed surveys and focus groups, was that Americans do trust libraries and expect them to serve as "a source of comfort in an age of anxiety" (*Buildings, Books, and Bytes*, 1996). Libraries have not disappeared as a result of the Internet, but the types of services provided and how spaces are used has changed dramatically. In a strategic plan, a library must study the types of technologically relevant services and spaces required by its user community.

Because technology plays such a central role in contemporary libraries, it is important that the systems office be involved in the planning process from the outset. Because of the enterprisewide role that the systems office plays, its members should collaborate widely with other units in the library on joint planning projects. Information technology, networked information, and new patterns of scholarly research are the just some of the issues driving strategic planning. There are rising and changing expectations about what comprises critical services; there are fewer resources with which to address those expectations. All of these factors suggest an evolving management model in libraries where strategic planning plays a key role. Forty-four Association of Research Libraries (ARL) institutions produced strategic plans in the early 1990s demonstrating broad acceptance of the process of strategic planning (Eustis & Kenney, 1996). Strategic planning helps libraries prioritize resource allocations. Therefore, strategic planning is a useful exercise for libraries whether external factors are driving the need for a plan or not. A business plan is a concrete reflection of the overall strategic planning process specifying the steps that will be taken to maximize resources. Bishoff and Allen (2004) offer a framework for developing business plans in libraries and other cultural institutions.

Policy Development

Policies articulate the mission of the library in a more granular way. Policies reflect shared values and define the scope of service that a library hopes to provide. Policies ensure that resources are effectively and equitably distributed across the organization. Policies should be nondiscriminatory and address broad issues. Avoid writing a policy that addresses the behavior of one or two people (Barclay, 2000). When individual problems arise, they can usually be handled as personnel matters, through employee coaching or evaluation procedures. Establish a periodic review process for all policies. Some employees may perceive the existence of policies as constricting, rigid, or inflexible, but good policies actually help people succeed in their jobs by establishing guidelines and maximizing the resources available to the library.

If your organization is hierarchical, involve all supervisors and use the correct channels to establish and communicate policy. A more negotiated process is necessary when your organization is team based. The majority of those responding to the Leung and Bisom (1996) survey involved a cross-section of faculty and staff, legal counsel, senior administrators, and students in their policy decisions. Policies can be controversial yet are often agents of change. Consider the organizational culture, traditions, and values affecting your particular institution to ensure relevant policies. Build consensus by keeping interaction focused on shared goals and outcomes.

In a typical hierarchical library, staffing levels are often set uniformly across operating units, reflecting the agendas of unit heads instead of real operating efficiencies (Gorman, 1987). In an information technology organization, decision making ought to distinguish clearly between policy and technical questions. The systems unit needs to understand this distinction. Technical decisions address whether a computer *can* perform a particular task. Policy decisions focus on whether a computer *should* perform a given task (McDonald, 1991).

Organizational stakeholders must be held accountable for the policy decisions they make that affect their libraries. For example, catalogers should be held responsible for the way records are loaded into the online catalog; reference librarians should be held responsible for decisions about screen displays. These kinds of decisions should not be politically motivated, that is, exercise power or control, but should be made in careful consideration of the institutional mission of the library.

All organizations are subject to the influences of politics. Libraries are no exception. For the sake of this discussion, we define *politics* as the exercise of power or control. Politics in this sense might refer to either internal or external forces vying for power or control. As an example of external politics affecting an organization, it took sixty-nine years after planning was complete to erect a new central facility for the Chicago Public Library. The delay was attributed to a shifting political climate in the city.

Communication is key to effective policy enforcement. Use the library intranet for publishing internal policies as well as serving as a central location so that all staff can locate them. This adds the advantage of making the content keyword searchable. Leung and Bisom (1996) found in their survey of ARL libraries that electronic means of disseminating policies such as handbooks and policy manuals were quickly superceding distribution in traditional paper formats. A printed manual probably is not the best method of communicating policies related to electronic information sources. All policies related to electronic information sources must, of course, be in line with the policies of the larger organization.

Several issues are of crucial importance to library systems and digitization initiatives: equitable and appropriate computer use, privacy, copyright, fair use, and fees (Graham, 1995). Make sure electronic information policies and disclaimers are consistent with existing policies, for example, codes of conduct, state law, privacy policies, intellectual ownership, and principles of intellectual freedom. These policies can affect not only library staff but also in-house and remote users. Information technology policies are key library policies in an age of electronic access. The impetus for addressing information technology policies may need to come from the systems office. Some policies may stem from the campus or university level, and the systems office might need to determine how to apply them in the library by, for example, creating procedures in support of the policy. Because libraries focus more directly on information, policies may also originate there and flow up to the college or university information technology units. This opportunity to shape and influence organizational policy must be clearly communicated and endorsed at each level.

One suggestion is to start from a draft statement. Begin by researching written policies that may have been developed in libraries similar to yours. A good starting place is the ARL's SPEC kits. These publications combine survey information and sample documents from research libraries to provide snapshots of current policies and practices. Recent executive summaries are available online at http://www.arl.org/spec/speclist.html. A draft should be discussed with the library director, systems staff, and the policy-making group within the library, if one exists. Follow through with revisions until there is an officially endorsed written policy. Make sure new policies are incorporated into the existing corpus of policy documents, such as what might be included in an employee handbook or new employee orientation materials. In some cases, the signature of a new employee might be desirable as a method of making sure new employees read the policy.

For public access computers, informing people about policies is trickier. There will be occasions when you'll need to post signs at each workstation. Large numbers of signs on a workstation decreases the likelihood that anybody will read them. You might post a more prominent sign at the entrance or on bulletin boards in the building. Ensure that all public services personnel are aware how IT-specific policies might affect users. Instruction librarians should be encouraged to explain policy implications in classroom sessions. Consider articles in campus publications or a Web site posting. Many universities have mechanisms to send mass e-mail to all students, faculty, and staff. The use of portals for this function is also gaining popularity because of the ability to target a specific audience segment. Either of these methods has the potential to provide an effective method for communicating policies that affect the entire university community, as well as the process or rationale behind the development of the policy. Libraries often develop policies to allocate finite resources fairly. It helps people accept new rules if they understand this. Always keep written policies accessible to users. Enforce policies as equitably as possible for all populations of users. When writing policies, be sure to include original approval dates as well as dates for any policy revisions. In the future, you might need to determine when a particular policy was put into force.

Budget

Plain talk about money can be a delicate issue in some libraries, whether in favorable or poor economic climates. Traditionally, library directors hold primary responsibility for the budget-planning process. Systems librarians have become more involved in the librarywide budget process because they spend a significant portion of it on creating and maintaining networked systems (Lavagnino, 1997, pp. 226–27). Lobby to establish a budget line for the information technology unit. Managers can be more effective in their planning efforts when they know in advance what budget is available. As noted in the Introduction to Muir's 1995 survey, "several sites mentioned an increasing need for the library systems office to have a role in the strategic and budgetary planning process not only of the library, but also at the university level." Parkhurst (1990) identifies budget preparation for projects as a function required of the systems office (p. 96). Working with budgets, you will soon discover that a firm grasp of spreadsheet software is invaluable.

It is worth the effort to understand the administration of the library budget when considering an employment offer. In some libraries, the systems office makes only purchase recommendations. In others, the systems office authorizes expenditures. Each library operates within a different framework of centralized, decentralized, or hybrid budget practices. If budget control is extremely decentralized, the systems office may have an easier time with its own purchasing, but units outside of systems might also elect to purchase hardware or software without approval and then expect assistance. Decide whether you can be effective under whatever circumstances you might encounter. Budget administration also affects the ability of the systems librarian to negotiate employment offers to systems staff. Find out whether you will have the ability to make last-minute or emergency purchases with minimal delays, or if you will need to wait for a formal annual review process. It may help you to read *Budgeting: A How-To-Do-It Manual for Librarians*, by Alice Warner (1998).

Planning Tools

Fashions in planning tools come and go. Often these ideas originate in the business sector and include such approaches as the Critical Path Method (CPM), total quality management (TQM), program evaluation and review technique (PERT), Gantt charts, systems analysis, reengineering, and surveys. Myllis (1990) describes the utilization in Finland of a planning method called METO, which was used to resolve specific problems of workflow and inefficient information services. Translated to English, the acronym METO stands for Information Systems Analysis Method. Planning tools can be useful for a variety of tasks including personnel effectiveness, resource analysis and evaluation, user perceptions, and cost estimates. Choosing an appropriate planning tool can help organize all of the data elements needed to obtain intelligible results. Learning to use a particular planning tool usually requires an investment of some study or research.

The benefits of using a proven planning tool will make the effort worthwhile in the long run. By incorporating good planning tools into the process, you can focus on attaining your stated goals and objectives.

Computer software programs such as Microsoft Project can help automate planning processes; a spreadsheet program, such as Microsoft Excel, is often used to estimate or track project costs. It is useful to be conversant with the array of planning tools available, so that you will be able to utilize them when appropriate. Excel and Project can also assist in developing reports or charts, which can be incredibly useful tools for introducing new initiatives to the library as a whole. These can be incorporated into presentations or written documents to clarify the planning strategy.

Systems analysis theory postulates congruence among four interacting components: work accomplished, characteristics of individuals, formal processes, and informal relationships (Huston & Grahn, 1991, pp. 40–41). There are a number of models that can be used in system analysis. What they have in common is that when one component changes, other elements are influenced to seek equilibrium. This approach is useful because it considers both the technical and social energies that can lead to planning successful change.

User feedback as a tool for planning has a long tradition in academic libraries. Surveys are a valid research methodology, but their validity is often reduced by unsophisticated construction. Surveys can be useful in assessing the direction of a library and evaluating effectiveness in meeting its mission, or they can simply measure user perceptions. An incorrectly constructed survey can make the responses invalid, so it is a good idea to find an expert to help with survey construction. One of the most common errors is to neglect the randomness of the sample population. The method in which surveys are distributed has been shown to influence the response data, so make sure to use an appropriate sampling technique. For some examples of survey construction, look at the public opinion survey reproduced in the appendix of *Buildings, Books, and Bytes*. The ARL SPEC kit 205 also provides some useful models.

There are also opportunities to outsource user surveys or utilize a commercial survey tool like Survey Monkey which includes built-in survey development assistance. You may be able to dedicate more time to analyzing the data by relying on an outside survey service, rather than building a new tool of your own. The campus may also support an office whose function includes assessment or survey support. The best outsourced surveys can effectively study concerns that are common to many different libraries. LibQUAL+ is a research and development project jointly sponsored by ARL and Texas A&M University that has been studying service quality across a broad array of institutions for several years. Although the focus of the survey is on services traditionally considered to be "public services," some of the questions in LibQUAL surveys do address technology in libraries. Participating in a consortial survey such as LibQUAL allows the library to gather important data about its own services. The library can also obtain comparison data to provide indicators of how it compares to peer organizations.

After collecting survey data, it will need careful and systematic analysis; scanning the data set can lead you to untenable or incorrect conclusions. Research methods coursework and a basic statistics course are valuable assets. Library schools might require a statistics course. If you haven't had a course, there may be continuing education opportunities on the campus that can help provide a basic understanding. Some universities also have departments that will support librarians and faculty in statistical analysis.

Cost analysis is a formal approach to comparing costs to benefits. It's possible to express cost analysis as a cost-to-benefit ratio. A spreadsheet can help you visualize these ratios. Figure 1.1 represents models for the basic considerations for cost-effectiveness.

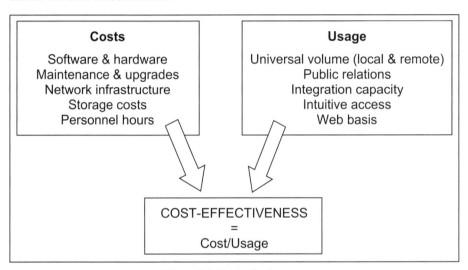

Figure 1.1. Cost-effectiveness.

Wilson (1998) nicely illustrates a formula to determine the total cost of your computers:

1. Add wages and benefits for systems staff, all training costs, the estimated annual cost for all repairs, and hardware and software upgrades.

2. Calculate the annual cost of learning something new by multiplying the number of nonsystems employees by about 5.1 hours a week by the average hourly wage by fifty-two weeks.

3. Divide the sum of Steps 1 and 2 by the total number of computers.

4. Divide the original cost of the computer by the estimated number of years of service.

5. Subtract results of Step 4 from the results of Step 3.

The result from Step 5 represents the total cost per computing machine per year.

Writing a Technology Plan

Technology plans help clarify and specify the goals of the systems office in relation to the strategic plan of the library. A technology plan is a hands-on guide to specific, short-term technology directions. Like the strategic plan, key elements might include a mission statement, goals, objectives, and costs. An IT strategic plan is broader and might not be granular enough to include specifics such as equipment purchases, hardware and software specifications, security, and disaster sections. Because technology changes quickly, a technology plan addresses shorter periods—from one to three years—so that it can be flexible enough for periodic review and adaptation. Strategic plans provide broad directions for the library. A technology plan can help the library determine the best way to use technology to meet the directions of the strategic plan.

Many systems offices developed a beginning basis for their technology plan as they prepared for the year 2000 (Y2K). Although a crisis never materialized, part of the reason may be attributable to the planning that preceded it. Consider how much risk your organization is willing to tolerate when incorporating new technology solutions in a technology plan. A leading-edge idea may not always result in success, but it can be a valuable learning experience for systems staff. The technology plan should reflect careful consideration of each variable but should be flexible enough to respond quickly to situational changes. Imhoff (1996) provides detailed instructions for developing a technology plan. The technology plan can be effective when it's tied to an annual departmental reporting process. This link provides an opportunity to assess how well goals and costs from the prior year were met while making realistic adjustments for the year to come. TechSoup, a national nonprofit technology assistance agency, provides planning guidelines, sample plans, and other useful documentation for getting started with a technology plan (http://www.techsoup.org/howto/articles.cfm?topicid=11&topic=Technology%20Planning).

Project Management

Projects are distinct from tasks in their greater complexity. Projects involve sets of tasks that are dependent on the successful completion of a series of steps; tasks are discreet events accomplished in a brief amount of time. Leonard (1993) identified project management as the most important skill requirement for a new systems librarian (p. 115). Specifically, the skill set includes the ability to coordinate projects effectively and establish project goals, budgets, and timelines. The systems librarian isn't alone in project management. A key element in successfully completing projects is collaboration with library or campus colleagues. Collaboration is essential to ensure the project meets the library or departmental service goals. Identify the steps needed to attain each goal and assign responsibility for its completion. Chu (1990) observes that "it is necessary to understand which processes can run in parallel and which ones are sequential" (p. 97). Project management software provides a visual representation of the sequence and dependencies of the required steps. Refer to the earlier discussion in the "Planning Tools" section of this chapter for more information and recommendations on specific software packages that can assist in project management.

Time management is an essential skill associated with project management because efficiently run projects always operate within a timeline. Although "technology places unseen demands on time: hidden time needs, instructional needs, and maintenance needs" (Walster, 1993, p. 5), there are numerous books and short courses that offer tools and insight to improve time management skills. "There are five basic components of a successful time management system: motivation, awareness of your time-use style, analysis procedures, implementation techniques, and planning strategies" (Walster, p. 18). Because time is a limited resource, the amount of time you spend on a project should reflect your commitment to the value of the project. Consult the bibliography in the Walster volume for additional resources.

Statistics and Decision Making

Libraries are not always statistics-driven organizations. Much routine data collection occurs, such as the number of titles cataloged in a given year. As libraries engage in strategic and other planning activities, statistics can play a significant and concrete role in decision making. The systems office often has responsibility for collecting general statistical information relating to library technology. Some statistical data are reported to external agencies, but other data can be useful in-house.

One example of an external body that collects statistical information about libraries is the Integrated Postsecondary Education Data System (IPEDS), which has collated data from libraries since 1986. Like its predecessor, the Higher Education General Information Survey (HEGIS), IPEDS is managed by the National Center for Education Statistics, a branch of the U.S. Department of Education. The IPEDS survey is a comprehensive tool that gathers institution-level data about all organizations that provide postsecondary education. The data sets can be used to study trends in higher education at local, state, or national levels (http://nces.ed.gov/ipeds/AboutIPEDS.asp). For this survey, the systems office may need to provide information regarding the number of computers in use, network connections, installed software, and other related information. Gathering this data is easier if systems staff have kept an accurate inventory database. See the "Inventory" section of Chapter 8 for ideas on managing equipment inventory data. There is an interactive comparison of data submitted by institutional respondents available on the Internet at http://nces.ed.gov/ipedspas.

The ARL also collects a variety of statistics from its member libraries that attempt to describe and measure the "performance of research libraries and their contribution to teaching, research, scholarship, and community service" (http://www.arl.org/stats/index.html). The statistics gathered cover general topics such as numbers of volumes and staff, specific studies of salaries, special libraries (such as law and medical libraries), and preservation practices. Each member library generally has a coordinator who is responsible for completing these surveys. The systems librarian can expect to be called on to answer questions or questionnaires that are specific to information technology. An overview of ARL's Statistics and Measurement Program is available online at http://www. arl.org/stats.

The statistics reported to external agencies are useful for broad, interinstitutional comparison. For more granular analysis and decision making, a variety of in-house or local statistics might be generated. These in-house statistics will come from a variety of sources. As Hawks (1988) points out, a fundamental role of the integrated library system should be to "provide management information to aid in decision making" (p. 131). Hawks identifies five sources of routine data in automated library systems. These include fund accounting, vendor performance, collection management, order control, and systems management. Think of Hawks's collection management category as inventory control, and it is clear that these management data have long been common in nonlibrary environments (Lancaster & Sandore, 1997, p. 48). Inventory control is an essential part of the business plan for retailers and manufacturers of all sizes. It is a key element for increasing the bottom line. Libraries should utilize inventory control to meet service goals and expectations. Lancaster and Sandore further observe that library vendors may not fully appreciate the value of the data that management reports can provide. This might be the case for some library integrated systems vendors, but others are at the forefront of providing invaluable statistical reports or the tools to generate your own.

Several authors suggest that more detailed library management reports would be useful. The systems department may utilize data from a variety of sources to generate reports, among them the online catalog system. Increasingly, decisions relating to the cost of purchasing electronic resources make it imperative to avoid duplication in electronic sources supplied by aggregators. In the past, this has been accomplished by overlap studies in which much of the analysis was done manually using conspectus lists. According to White (1990), the statistical reporting tools built into integrated library systems do not address every need, so local applications are often designed. This may hold true for a number of reasons. First, not all vendors realize how important system data are to the decision-making process within the library and thus neglect to provide adequate appropriate statistics. In cases when adequate data are provided, the reports available within the software may not develop them into easily understood formats. Additionally, each organization may require data unique to their own circumstances. When developing in-house statistical reports, always keep in mind that the cost of collecting and analyzing data should never exceed its utility.

When providing an in-house report, it is useful to provide an interpretation rather than just the raw data generated by the application. Data must generate information, but information must undergo transformation before it becomes useful knowledge. The ability of the systems librarian to use tools such as Excel will ease the process of making sense of numbers. This skill can also help to transform the data into reports with a user-friendly format. Nevertheless, just because the numbers make sense to you does not ensure they will to a colleague. Familiarize yourself with the elements of the *executive summary.* An executive summary is usually no longer than 10 percent of the original report and helps the reader make sense of the data. It summarizes the details of the report and helps place it in context. Many readers will not or cannot take the time to digest a report carefully. The executive summary should highlight the most important or significant findings. It might also make recommendations based on the findings. The business and technical writing literature is filled with descriptions of executive summaries and "how-to" methods that can assist in preparing such a document.

Integrated Library System Migration

It is nearly impossible to imagine a library systems career without at least one encounter with system migration. During the 1980s and early 1990s, many libraries were still implementing their first integrated system. Many libraries have migrated multiple times since then. Libraries change systems for many reasons. Once you begin weighing the options offered by vendors, it will quickly become clear that no one offers the perfect solution. There is risk in migrating, but there is also risk in remaining with some vendor systems. "More than a score of vendors have failed in the past 25 years" (Boss, 1997, p. 145). In a subsequent personal communication (November 20, 2003), Boss notes that "the pattern has changed to one of vendors purchasing weak competitors. For example, Sirsi purchased DRA, which previously had purchased INLEX and MultiLis. At least six companies that would have failed in time were purchased by competitors in the past five years." The fact that so much turnover exists in the vendor marketplace is an indication of how much study, analysis, and thought is required for this important decision-making process. Furthermore, it gives an idea of just how quickly the market changes even for software as specialized as ILS systems. Marshall Breeding's Library Technology Guides (http://www.librarytechnology.org) offers up-to-date news about the current ILS marketplace and other useful resources such as links to vendors and trend analyses.

Today, most libraries that implement a new system are migrating from an older system. Cronin (1989) suggested several questions to address during system migration: "What worked well the first time? What needs to be improved? How can this system's implementation be better for both library staff and users?" (p. 76). A library is likely to have many additional questions as well that are specific to its own environment. It is important to review work flow and policy at some time during this process. Stay focused on ways in which current ways of doing things could be transformed into more efficient procedures instead of perpetuating current practice for its own sake.

Migration to a new integrated library system is costly, so, from the point of view of the systems office, what factors should precipitate change? Machovec (1991) offers some technical justifications: the existing hardware platform is inadequate or is no longer being supported by the manufacturer, software enhancements are not available, major unresolved software problems persist, and resource sharing capability is lacking. According to Peters (1988), there are three major concerns when evaluating a system: functional, economic, and performance evaluation. These three criteria operate in sequence. Libraries will purchase a system if it is unique and affordable. They compare costs when two systems have approximately the same functionality. If function and cost are similar, then the third criterion is applied and performance becomes the decision point. Brown (1988) describes an early experience of stress testing, which might be a consideration if the selected ILS vendor has no prior experience installing large or specialized systems. A further technical consideration is the level of work required in the systems office for initial programming and profiling as well as software installation.

The integrated library system might seem like such a fundamental component of operation that many libraries might never address the true costs associated with managing such a system. R2 Consulting Services was recently contracted by a vendor to study the cost and impact of implementing, owning, and managing the ILS. Their white paper makes it clear that the price of purchasing and maintaining a system is just one part of the overall cost. A variety of hidden costs can greatly increase the total cost of ownership of the ILS. The study encourages librarians to think beyond the visible costs of the ILS and consider these hidden costs such as the amount of time spent designing profiles or generating custom reports. Workflow in libraries can also have a great impact on the real cost of an ILS. All of these issues need to be studied when considering migration to a new system (Lugg & Fischer, 2003).

Contemporary integrated library system software can be provided as a "turnkey" system. In this scenario, the vendor provides complete system setup and, sometimes, also the required equipment. Vendors may also market individual system elements separately and allow the library to run this software on the platform of their choice. Most systems allow a significant degree of customization even within the turnkey model to meet customers' individual requirements. Nevertheless, a turnkey environment is a practical and cost-effective option for many libraries. In the past, librarians struggled with some systems and spent hours debugging lines of code, documenting faulty modules, or working on the telephone with a system vendor to determine fixes. ILS software today is based on industry standards, and often times libraries have more control of their systems than in the past. Vendors provide better documentation and a wide variety of online resources to assist in supporting ILS systems. It is difficult to imagine hiring an

IT staff with sufficient expertise to support an ILS fully. In a large library with a great deal of support, it might be advantageous to install the ILS software on locally managed servers. A client/server environment, in which software processing tasks are split between the client (local computer) and server, is becoming increasingly prevalent in the ILS marketplace. This model differs from legacy ILS systems in which all processing occurred on the server.

Some vendors sell ILS software based on the Oracle platform, and others offer systems built on proprietary databases. Oracle, an industry standard, offers a great deal of flexibility, particularly in report creation. If the organization has the expertise to run a system that is Oracle based, explore the potential benefits of having more local control of your ILS. Above all, throughout the selection process it is essential to weigh the advantages and disadvantages of various vendors to determine the best and most appropriate solution for your organization. Beyond the technical requirements of the system, the library should consider what type of relationship they will enter with a turnkey vendor. Good communication and a strong customer service outlook on the vendor's part will greatly ease the library's ability to support a turnkey system.

The systems office could never hope to accomplish a major migration project without broad participation. The library administration must demonstrate strong support for the migration itself as well as the leadership efforts of the systems office. It must also play a key role in developing enthusiasm across the organization and recruiting qualified participants from a variety of departments and units. Involve as many staff members as possible early in the process, and everyone will have a chance to learn the system incrementally and become expert more quickly. Such involvement can also enhance the development of a broader, ongoing training agenda as the system is deployed in the library. Vendor documentation can be technical and exhaustive. It can be more readily distilled into crib sheets and departmental or module-based manuals when people get a chance to work with it early in the process. The systems librarian might have little experience with the day-to-day minutia of specific system modules or the workflow details that could impact system profiling and ongoing performance. As a generalist, it is inconceivable that one individual could know everything about every module. There are great benefits if the staff members who will use the module are involved in training. Those who use the system daily best understand (or need to understand) the quirks and intricacies of the software. If involved in training, staff members will feel they have a stake in the system. This buy-in will make migration easier and might even lead to innovative use of the system throughout its lifetime.

Another important consideration in system migration is the public interface or the public access catalog. Good interfaces facilitate the interaction of people and computers. Screen display, navigation, design options, library branding, and personalization are all important considerations when assessing the public interface. This raises the many challenges of screen design. Prior to Web-based public catalogs, online public access catalog (OPAC) designers were often limited to a certain number of characters per line and a set number of lines per screen. Long ago Machovec (1991) prescribed a menu-driven interface for novices and a command-line interface for experienced users (p. 39), but later Negroponte (1995) argued it was simply pedantic to "stubbornly [try] to make dumb machines easier to use by smart people" (p. 94). He suggested that the secret to good interface design was to "make it go away" (p. 93), or in other words, that the interface should be invisible to the user. In less than a decade, all of this has changed thanks to graphical user interfaces. The advent of the World Wide Web and Web-based public catalogs has to some extent accomplished exactly what Negroponte wished. The library Web catalog should ideally have a professional look and feel. Designers should rely on industry standards to ensure compatibility with the most commonly available Web browsers. The transition from character-based to graphical interfaces has dramatically changed the user experience in libraries.

Because report creation is a vital function of the ILS, it is important to evaluate a system's reporting capabilities when migrating. These reports will be useful for the typical library statistics-reporting functions but can also be indicators or how the system is performing. It will likely be the systems librarian's responsibility to schedule, run, and retain some of these reports as well as to interpret the data produced for colleagues.

Reports generated by library software typically include statistical reports, exception reports, customized on-demand reports, and predictive reports. Statistical reports are typically frequency counts, summaries of system activity, or ratios. A frequency count might be a report of the number of books checked in or checked out or how many times a particular electronic reserve item was viewed by a given class. Systems activity reports might track numbers of transactions or logins. Exception reports point to issues in workflow or processing that occur outside of an expected parameter, such as a date. Circulation override reports, duplicate record reports, or authority control exception reports are examples. Custom reports answer specific questions but are not routinely run. Examples of this type might include a fund report generated to indicate the amounts spent in certain accounts or a listing of malfunctioning URLs. Predictive reports project current data into the future and can be helpful in identifying emerging trends that may have an impact on such areas as allocation for staffing, budget, or access points. They can also help evaluate the effectiveness of current policies. System statistics help identify areas for which publicity, promotion, or user education may be beneficial. They can aid in projecting budget needs and predicting the effects of inflation. Reports also help maintain catalog integrity and examine catalog usage, design, and workstation placement. As noted earlier in the chapter, a basic statistics class is an asset in understanding certain types of reports because it can provide a basis for a conceptual understanding of the meaning hidden in the data. Facility with statistics provides insight into the answers that data can supply, as well as how much confidence to place in the results.

An ongoing task in system migration is the management and preparation of vendor proposals and contracts. Cortez (1987) specifically discusses the preparation of ILS proposals and contracts. His book provides examples of technical and functional specifications to use in a request for proposal (RFP) or a request for quotation (RFQ). An RFI is simply a request for information. Both Pitkin (1991) and Boss (1997) provide detailed criteria for each step in the process of system selection. *Library Technology Reports* (*LTR*) periodically targets an issue on the selection and migration process. Nicole Waller's (2003) *LTR* issue focused on a model RFP. Marshall Breeding's (2004) *LTR* is a guide to the ILS marketplace. For general information and sample RFPs, you may wish to consult http://www.ilsr.com/sample.htm. Your library may wish to hire a specialist to guide you through the process. A brief list of Web sites that will guide you to library automation consultants appears in "Resource Materials" at the end of the book. Most institutions have stringent policies and guidelines for purchases of this magnitude. Because of the institution-specific nature of purchasing and the legal contracts involved, a close collaboration with several university offices outside of the library is required.

Local Standards

A standard is "something established for use as a rule or basis of comparison in measuring or judging capacity, quantity, content, value, or quality" (Michael & Hinnebusch, 1995, p. 11). MARC, Z39.50, Open System Interconnection (OSI), and Transmission Control Protocol/Internet Protocol (TCP/IP) are important examples of widely practiced standards in the development of library technology. A hallmark of the exponential growth in technology is that standards have developed, in most cases, more slowly than the technologies themselves. Innovators explore areas in which standards are not yet established. When standards do not yet exist, libraries frequently develop local standards to which everyone in the organization is expected to adhere. Once a standard is endorsed, however, libraries should reevaluate their local practices. Each library will need to assess how to apply national standards locally. The result of this might be an adjustment to local practices affecting anything from record creation to workflow. An appropriate application of national standards will facilitate future migration between systems and permit sharing of data between otherwise unrelated systems. The systems librarian should know how to find information on standards and be prepared to put them into context for colleagues. Refer to the section called "Impacts and Applications of International Standards" in Chapter 10 for additional information about selected information standard organizations.

Libraries have a tradition of standards because they share a key professional value in the sharing of information. Standards improve interoperability and facilitate information sharing in a logical, organized, and predictable fashion. MARC is the most familiar example of a library standard. Since the early 1970s, the MARC Z39.2 standard has specified predictable fields for bibliographic data.

"Prior to . . . MARC, there were multiple formats used for bibliographic description. It was with the acceptance of the MARC standardization format that thousands of libraries, instead of producing their own catalog cards, ordered uniform cards through the [Library of Congress] Card Distribution Center" (Imhoff, 1996, p. 5). Libraries that hesitated to give up local practices and conform to the MARC standard had the most difficulty and expense converting their records into formats that could be easily used by ILS vendors. Adherence to local practices after a standard has been codified is more commonly found in nonacademic environments, making multitype collaborative projects much more complicated and cumbersome when they have been attempted.

Replacement Cycles

Equipment purchasing cycles are driven by the dynamic between software and hardware developers. As technologies such as memory chips, disk input/output speed (I/O), and processors have matured, software developers have been motivated to write more powerful programs that take advantage of them. To utilize the powerful, new software tools, libraries must purchase bigger, faster machines. Most libraries are unable to accumulate funds over more than one fiscal year to replace all of their installed equipment at once. It is also unlikely to have sufficient staffing in place to replace the entire installed equipment base in a single year. Therefore, the systems office must systematically plan for periodic equipment rotation. Seek input from library staff early in the process to minimize friction and allow all stakeholders to point out any oversights in the purchasing process. "Thoughtful LAN [local area network] administrators rely on input from end users and librarians to learn of specific needs and problems with the system so that an informed judgment can be made about an upgrade. This is how LAN administrators not only keep their networks current and functional, but also keep the network's users satisfied" (Corbly, 1997, pp. 195–96). As a rule of thumb, consider the life expectancy of a computer to be between three and five years. Several factors will influence this. Public machines, for example, might need minimal computing power but are regularly in use nearly every day of the year for twelve or more hours a day. Some staff, such as Web designers, will need computers with cutting-edge technologies, large amounts of memory, and powerful processors. By balancing all of the needs, you can develop a cycle that best fits your organization. The formula illustrated in Figure 1.2 may prove useful in determining your annual budget request for computers.

[Total of All Installed Computers]

÷ [Years of Estimated Life]

= [Number of Computers to Purchase Annually]

Then Take

[Number of Computers to Purchase Annually]

x [Average Computer Cost, e.g., $2000]

= [Annual Computer Budget]

Figure 1.2. Computer rotation budget.

The annual budget number is likely to be a large one. How do you justify such a request each year? Dvorak (1995), basing his estimate on a $3,000 computer, suggests that "over two years, a new PC works out to about $4 a day for a tool that is critical to most people's work" (p. 89). A computer with sufficient power for most library needs in 2004 costs approximately $1,500. Following Dvorak's formula, the capital outlay for a computer today works out to about $2 per day. This is a relatively low expense considering that computing is an essential piece of the infrastructure of doing business in a library. To stretch budget dollars farther, consider purchasing discounted equipment when a manufacturer discontinues a model line, but verify both that it will meet existing needs and that the vendor will continue to support it. Midrange equipment might have the computing power you need at a more cost-effective price point. Remember that large purchases are often eligible for a volume discount, so if you can purchase in bulk, it has the potential to result in better pricing than many state or educational price contracts. Academic institutions also qualify for educational discounts and are usually tax exempt, so online pricing information will not always apply to your situation. Vendor, computer industry, and publisher Web sites do provide useful guidelines for estimating costs, however. One example is the CNET Review site (http://reviews.cnet.com). It is also good practice to cultivate personal relationships with regional vendor representatives. Major manufacturers and resellers often have one employee who works exclusively with educational institutions. That person can provide invaluable advice about which models are intended for the consumer market and which are designed for enterprise applications. Individual manufacturers may have a Web site dedicated to educational purchasing. Don't forget to determine whether and how shipping costs will affect your purchasing ability.

The university's purchasing office will usually have rules and procedures for large equipment purchases. Written justification is necessary for large equipment expenditures in some libraries. Sometimes these are regulated by a process of receiving bids from vendors, so be sure to provide detailed specifications to the purchasing office to ensure that the computers you eventually receive will meet your needs. Include specific information about service requirements and coverage you expect from the vendor. Otherwise, you may find your time wasted in boxing-up computers to ship them somewhere or waiting for a return merchandise authorization (RMA) from the vendor. You might also incur shipping and insurance costs in these circumstances. If you order large numbers of machines, be sure to plan ahead and prepare to receive, unpack, and store multiple units.

When the purchasing office receives bids from vendors, they will usually award the contract to the lowest bidder. Typically, a purchase order (PO) is then sent to that vendor. If you take the time to do preliminary pricing with vendors, verify that they will accept purchase orders. If you need to meet a fiscal spending deadline, confirm with vendors that your order is in stock, or at least that they can guarantee a delivery date. When the vendor receives the PO, it will then ship the equipment and invoice the university. When the invoice is paid, the university usually attaches an inventory tag to the equipment. It is useful to record PO numbers, institutional inventory tag numbers, date received, model information, and serial numbers in your library equipment database for future reference. Fill out any warranty cards and register your purchase with the vendor to make certain you will receive any necessary service on your equipment during the warranty period specified in your purchase agreement.

Disaster Preparedness and Recovery

Libraries generally have an established set of emergency procedures. Some campuses require departments and units to have disaster plans and provide guidelines and planning tools. The systems office should participate fully in the development and review of these procedures as they apply to computer equipment. Most institutions wrote extensive procedures in the months before the year 2000, preparing for exigencies which never materialized, but these documents might be valuable as a starting point for future disaster planning efforts. Periodically, verify that all emergency contact information is current in any written documentation.

In formulating emergency procedures, anticipate natural disasters such as fire, flood, and electrical failure and formalize the steps required under each scenario. Backup power generators are expensive, but you can easily install uninterruptible power supplies, especially on any mission-critical servers. You can build them into the purchase package in most cases. In addition, install the appropriate software on each server that will close down server processes and shut the machine off correctly in the event of a power failure.

Fire extinguishers should be available in proximity to servers. There are several kinds of extinguishers. The server room extinguisher must be appropriate for electrical fires. Verify that inspection stickers are up-to-date. Fire protection is likely something that the library can work on in collaboration with the campus fire marshal.

Disaster preparedness planning is distinct from disaster recovery. A business continuity plan (BCP) should be developed to delineate the steps required after a disaster occurs. Some universities have undertaken this kind of an exercise, which includes working through hypothetical scenarios to better prepare departments in case of a real emergency. A good BCP will indicate what staffing and resources are needed to get operations up and running after a disaster as well as specify what facilities and equipment are required in case existing infrastructure is damaged or unsafe. We have included an illustration of a questionnaire used to develop a BCP in the resource materials at the end of the book.

2

Staffing and Reporting Lines

Systems office organization is largely a function of your library environment and history, but it should be reexamined periodically. Reporting lines and staffing allocations should respond in dynamic ways to environmental changes. There are a variety of publications in the literature that have closely studied the organization of the systems office. One of the most interesting figures found in Leonard's 1993 report was that nearly "87 percent of respondents . . . showed library directors reporting to the Provost or to the Academic Vice President; none to the Computing Center" (p. 114). Nevertheless, close alliances between campus libraries and computer centers are likely today. If a formal reporting line connection doesn't exist between the library and the computer center, one can expect that there is a strong informal relationship. A 1986 ARL survey showed that in the United States, about 51.3 percent of systems librarians reported to the director. By 1991, that percentage had increased to 60 percent. In 1991, Muirhead (1994) found that 66.1 percent of British systems librarians also reported to the director (pp. 25–26). This is an indirect comparison, but these figures do seem to reflect an awareness of the librarywide responsibilities of the systems office. Even though the percentage of systems librarians reporting to library directors didn't change between 1991 and 2002, the executive summary of the ARL (Muir & Lim, 2002) SPEC Kit 271 indicates that duties and levels of responsibility are on the increase. The report concludes the current trend of systems offices reporting to the dean or director will continue (p. 10).

According to survey data collected by Muir (1995, Introduction), there was a 37 percent increase in the number of systems staff during the five-year period between 1990 and 1995, with the greatest increase being in the number of network specialists. This is to be expected, particularly because during this time, many libraries were making a transition from dumb terminals to personal computers. The raw data Muir supplied represent useful alternatives for considering the organization of the systems office. Research libraries confirmed this trend. Between 1994 and 2002, fifty-eight of sixty-one libraries reported that systems staff had grown. Staffing remained the same for the other three survey respondents. Supervision of staff consumes a significant portion of a manager's time. It is difficult for one person to supervise directly and effectively many more than seven to ten employees. If the systems staff has grown beyond this number, consider ways to redistribute supervisory responsibility among key members of the unit. Not coincidentally, the 2002 ARL study of system office organization found that 50 percent of systems offices had reorganized since 1994; this was, of course, just when the Internet started to impact library services (p. 9). Some reorganized due to larger reorganizations of the library. Others created new units or teams to tackle new technologies or programs. Because the workload continued to increase, some departments also placed increased reliance on other library departments or consortia (p. 13). The study also indicates that most systems offices allow staff to specialize. In many cases, technical staff is responsible for ongoing high-lever technical support while systems librarians focus on management issues (p. 11).

Libraries are chronically understaffed, and so optimize the potential contribution of every library staff member to the work of the systems office. Several time-saving technological innovations can also help save time and effort; for example, enable automatic update options on computer desktops and establish methods to keep desktop operating systems, browsers, and other software versions current. Decide whether systems staff should be centralized or distributed. A centralized staffing model facilitates response to a wide variety of calls throughout the library system but might neglect the specialized needs of branch libraries. Conversely, by relying on a distributed model, it could be more difficult to respond to needs that affect the enterprise as a whole. The most effective strategy might include a blend of both approaches. One strategy for extending limited central staff is to establish technical liaisons within each unit who are willing to participate in higher-level training opportunities. Keep in mind that if your systems unit is short of staff, other units probably are, too. Whatever approach is taken must benefit the entire library. The Michigan State Board of Education developed a staffing levels worksheet to determine the number of technology support staff needed in a school district. The worksheet, available at http://techguide.merit.edu/worksheet.htm, may be adaptable as a tool to help determine staffing needs in your library. Because most libraries rely heavily on delivering services from their Web sites, it may also be useful to consult the SPEC

Kit 266 (November 2001), *Staffing the Library Web site,* which reports on the ways in which ARL libraries allocate staff to support their Web presence.

If your library does not have a discrete systems office, the responsibility for its creation may someday be yours. Lavagnino (1998) outlines a four-step process that may prove useful. First, collect data that demonstrate need using interviews, observation, and logs. Second, organize and present preliminary data to stakeholders. Include examples, quotes, and stories to illustrate the data's significance. Prepare statistics for your own situation and benchmark them to peer libraries. Third, write a plan that identifies all of the necessary steps. The fourth step is implementation. It is also important to evaluate your progress at a specific point in time to reassess goals and priorities.

Gorman's (1987) pragmatic approach to staffing seems reductionistic but is offered here as a rule-of-thumb. He says,

- No professional should perform a paraprofessional task.

- No paraprofessional should perform a clerical task.

- No human should perform a task that can be done by a machine. (p. 158)

Due to short staffing in libraries and because staff generally maintain a strong public service outlook, it is often difficult to reassign tasks or even automate them. Above all else, the systems office must remain a strong advocate for automating all appropriate tasks if Gorman's advice is taken seriously.

It is common in the workplace for people to feel that they aren't appreciated. If you want to increase motivation, production, and staff retention, consider ways that you, as a manager, can frequently express your appreciation to your staff. This can take the form of a major event, a note, or just a short conversation. It isn't good practice to wait until the annual review period to let your staff members know they're appreciated for a number of reasons.

The Systems Librarian

Depending on the size of the library, it is likely that at least one individual will have the responsibilities and title of "systems librarian." As technology continues to permeate libraries, the number of systems librarians as well as their significance in the organization is likely to increase. The historical notes section of this book briefly covered the history of this relatively new discipline of librarianship. This section addresses the position of systems librarian in more detail and in the context of today's academic libraries.

The systems librarian is a unique breed. The position requires someone who not only understands libraries and computers but someone who can put both fields into context. There have been innumerable discussions ever since computers were first used in libraries whether systems librarians should be computer experts or computer experts with an understanding of libraries. Although the position responsibilities are often similar, the job title has varied greatly.

Sample job titles for librarians specializing in the area of library systems have included the following:

- Systems coordinator
- Systems librarian
- Head, electronic resources
- Head, networked information
- Head, computer services
- Microcomputer and instructional systems coordinator
- Coordinator of automated services
- Director of library systems
- Director of systems and support services
- Systems manager
- Automation services librarian
- LAN manager
- Networking librarian
- Online catalog librarian
- Instructional computing/technology consultant
- Electronic services librarian
- Systems analyst
- Networked systems specialist
- Programmer/analyst
- Information technology team leader

In her 1997 study of academic position advertisements, Foote found *systems librarian* to be the most common title, followed by *automation librarian,* and *systems coordinator.* Of the 107 job titles she identified, 51 were unique. What is it that a systems librarian does and what makes the job important? This, of course, differs widely depending on the size of the library as well as the services it offers. Most studies agree that integrated library systems management is a major responsibility. Other library servers, networks, and workstations claim an ever increasing amount of time, but the ILS will probably continue to be central as long as the library catalog is the primary finding tool for library materials. Although Foote's study clearly shows that libraries are looking for a librarian to manage the ILS, Dunsire (1994) cautions, "an immediate problem for the systems librarian is the perception and accepted definition of what constitutes the system" (p. 63). In one true incident, a director was trying to get a storage room organized and assigned the systems librarian to inventory "everything that plugged in."

There are many articles that analyze the desired characteristics of systems librarians in position announcements. Many of the traits are common to any library position. For example, many position announcements require interpersonal and communication skills, experience, and flexibility as a matter of course. Lavagnino (1997) identified the top skills required by a systems librarian as problem solving, planning, oral, interpersonal, organizational, and written communication, negotiating, and supervising (p. 227). Foote's (1997) study found that 75 percent of position announcements required experience with technology. This requirement is likely to increase until it becomes universal. Croneis and Henderson (2002) reviewed postings for electronic and digital librarians and found a marked increase in the demand for specialized skills such as the ability to manage electronic resources or digital initiatives projects.

Martin (1988) suggested a laundry list of tasks for systems librarians. With the possible exception of the importance of CD-ROM technologies, Martin's list, although fifteen years old, includes many of the skills still required by systems librarians in the Internet age and could well serve as a basic checklist.

- Remain current with evolving technology

- Maintain good working relationships with the campus computer center

- Provide technical support for online databases

- Support CD-ROM usage, development, and production

- Develop local databases

- Maintain cabling, gateways, and linked systems

- User support

- Expand the scope of the online catalog

- Study expert systems and artificial intelligence agents

Salaries for systems librarians vary from location to location. They are subject to the forces at play in the economy at large, years of experience, local budgets, and other factors. The salary range has changed significantly given the new responsibilities of serving as systems librarian in the Internet age. Salary also depends on the level of the position or appointment. Some systems librarians are senior management, and others are middle managers. Some have no supervisory responsibilities, whereas others might supervise technical staff or a combination of staff and other systems librarians.

The ARL publishes selected salary study results from its member institutions online at http://www.arl.org/stats/salary. The Association of College and Research Libraries (ACRL) also publishes salary information every other year in its Academic Library Trends and Statistics report at http://acrl.telusys.net/trendstat/2002.

Original contracts are generally negotiable. Carefully consider both your needs and the marketplace during the process of negotiating any offer. For comparative purposes, salary information for employees of public institutions is normally available on request, but tact is obviously advisable.

Wilson's 1998 volume, *The Systems Librarian*, does a comprehensive job of describing who the systems librarian is and what the position entails. The definition he offers is this: "systems librarians coordinate the effective use of technology throughout the organization regardless of the department concerned . . . [and] represents a blend of library science, computer operations, and management" (p. 11). He warns that practicing systems librarians struggle with poorly defined job descriptions, which can vary dramatically from library to library.

Teams and Hierarchies

Historically, academic libraries have often adopted hierarchical organizational schemes. Reporting responsibilities may be described in detailed tree diagrams known as organization charts (see "Organization Chart" later in the chapter), with decisions made at the top of the organization, normally by a dean or library director. Top-down decision making may be accompanied by a tradition of consensual decision making among the librarians, especially in the approximately 50 percent of academic libraries where the librarians hold faculty status. By the late 1980s, some were beginning to challenge this traditional organizational structure. For example, Gorman (1987) proposed that efficiency and humane treatment of all kinds of library employees could not be achieved within traditional hierarchical library structures because they strictly tie workers to a defined position, thus discouraging personal growth in the workplace.

Lancaster and Sandore (1997) discuss the ways in which technology has had a profound effect on the organizational structure of libraries. Libraries are now likely to have more participative management and diminished lines of command. Technology has also served to blur traditional boundaries and encourage wider utilization of issue-centered working groups or task forces. Several other authors have also studied the impact of technology on organizational change. De Klerk and Euster (1989) found libraries experimenting with a variety of organizational forms, with their goal being to increase flexibility to respond to technological change. The effectiveness and suitability of collaborative work was highlighted by Connell and Franklin (1994). Schwartz (1997) collected essays and case studies about technology-driven organizational change.

Sweeney (1994) cites technology as an influencing factor in what he terms the "posthierarchical" library. He favors flatter organizations and cross-functional teams focused on customer services. Teams are increasingly being established in academic libraries. They can be fairly static in their composition but sometimes are more fluid and task-centered in their formation. Mutually negotiated compromise is crucial in a team-based organization because there is both shared decision making and shared accountability for the success of each decision or initiative. Experts working in isolation are less effective than those who work in a team environment. The team facilitator must be aware of team members' different perspectives and keep their focus on the overall goal. For example, a systems team member might advocate for a lengthy testing period to ensure that a new technology works correctly. Someone more concerned with the content provided by the new technology might consider the test period a delay. The team facilitator must be able to forge a compromise. Team captains must possess an appreciation for communication, a commitment to conferring with stakeholders, the judgment to assign reasonable tasks, and the realism to set and achieve feasible time schedules—all within budget limitations.

Diversity of backgrounds and experience is desirable to ensure a variety of strengths among team members. The organization might decide to enhance teamwork through the use of tools like the Minnesota Multiphasic Personality Inventory (MMPI) and the Meyers-Briggs. These are commonly employed tools that may help staff appreciate the complementary approaches individuals bring to a group.

Teams and committees need clear charges to perform their work. They need to know the boundaries of their responsibility and when to involve another individual or group in a decision. Decision-making guidelines help clarify the roles of all participants in a team environment. The "Resource Materials" section at the end of the book provides a model decision-making tool.

Organization Charts

A visual representation of your library's reporting lines and staffing relationships can be informative, regardless of whether it is a traditional hierarchy, understood as a system, or structured around teams. Commonly used in the private sector, organization charts are valuable for both the library administration wishing to use staff more effectively and new employees who want to know who the key contact people are. In a 1996 survey by Eustis and Kenney (Introduction), the majority of responding ARL libraries had an organization chart of the library.

If an organization chart doesn't exist or is outdated, the systems office may take the initiative to develop one, but this might be challenging because academic libraries regularly use temporary committees or task forces to manage complex projects. The collaborative nature of these groups is difficult to portray on a formal, hierarchical organizational chart (De Klerk & Euster, 1989, p. 467). The systems office might not necessarily be represented explicitly within each of these groups, but their responsibilities cut across and influence every segment of the organization even if the chart does not illustrate the relationship.

Visio, the drawing component of Microsoft Office, is one example of a software program that can be used to create organization charts. This type of software may already be available in the systems office because it is useful for other purposes as well, for example, creating network diagrams. Some organizations use Microsoft PowerPoint for organization chart design. Others have found it effective to purchase a separate package altogether such as OrgPlus (http://www.orgplus.com). OrgPlus integrates with most human resources information systems to automatically generate organization charts from existing data as well as with Microsoft Office software for budgeting and presentation purposes.

Consult the ARL SPEC Kit 170 for samples of organization charts used at other institutions. The three figures that follow are examples of three ways to illustrate organizational relationships. The first is a traditional hierarchy (Figure 2.1), the second shows the interaction of each unit with the others (Figure 2.2), and the third is a hybrid of teams and reporting lines (Figure 2.3).

Centralization and Branches

In academic libraries, there can be widely differing philosophies in terms of centralized versus distributed service locations. The basic issues are certainly debated in larger theatres than libraries, ranging from effective government models to computer networking. Once a model is embraced, it becomes logistically and financially difficult to change course. Branch libraries are more common in larger universities than in smaller ones.

Some branch or departmental libraries can afford to cultivate or hire their own technical experts, but many rely on centrally located library technical support or campus computing centers. Staff in branches may tend to feel isolated or neglected by systems staff. Implement routine maintenance and training schedules for branch or departmental libraries or establish technical liaison relationships with a designated individual to help coordinate service and support in each location. It might even be possible to hire a student employee for this task, which could be accomplished in a few hours each week. The systems office might also opt to earmark some dedicated IT space in branch locations. This can serve as a staging or storage area or even a work space for systems staff in the field.

Geographically separated departmental libraries can be an effective way to target the needs of focused research populations but may present a special set of considerations for a central staff expected to provide technical support to many locations. This is not a new challenge. It is as true for central cataloging departments who provide support for many locations as it is for central systems departments. New technologies allow systems staff to monitor many computer activities centrally. Nevertheless, there are several instances in which a staff member needs to travel to a branch library site to work on a piece of equipment. In addition to technical support personnel, some of the efficiencies of equipment allocation are similar in nature to more traditional monographic and serial resources when branches are numerous. Some duplication of resources will inevitably exist. In some situations, resources may be available from the academic department to support a branch library.

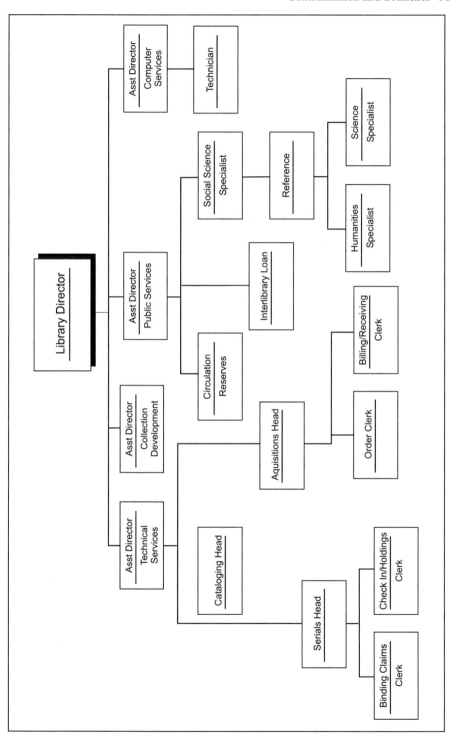

Figure 2.1. Organizational tree chart.

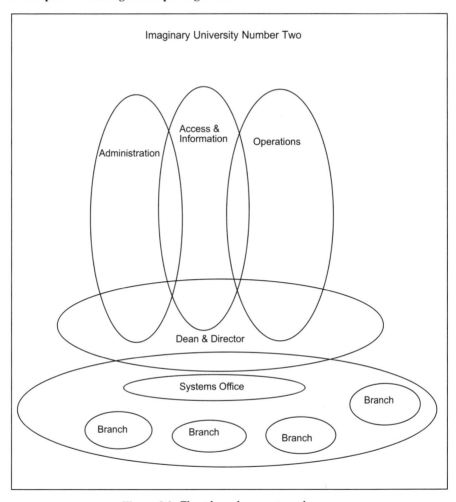

Figure 2.2. Chart based on system theory.

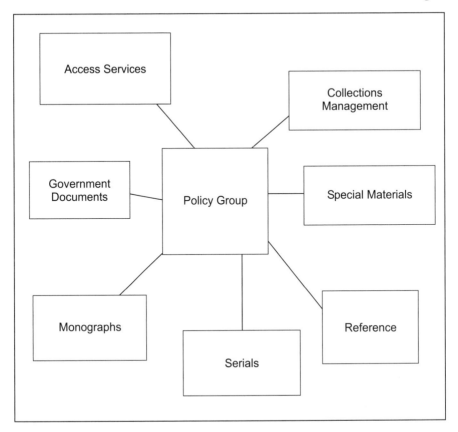

Figure 2.3. Team-based chart.

Telecommuting

Technology has created opportunities for libraries to enable employees to telecommute under certain circumstances. Telecommuting employees are dependent on reliable computer and network connectivity to be productive. Their situation is analogous in some ways to that in branch libraries. Sweeney (1994) advises that telecommuters must spend some time in the office to become better acquainted with on-site workers. Telecommuting employees must also have the authority to make decisions for their area even if they are not on-site. Technical support for telecommuters, as in the branch library discussion, should be proactive and systematic. It can also be problematic. Telecommuters who use library supplied and supported laptops make equipment maintenance a little easier, but what if the remote employee uses his or her own computer and expects support from the systems office? The systems office must clearly delineate the nature of support telecommuters can expect to receive. This necessarily will reflect the library's broader philosophy and support for workers in remote locations.

Telecommuting may also appeal to consultants, trainers, or other systems related specialists because they don't have to be physically available to one organization exclusively. You may be able to delegate some work—for example, Web maintenance—to this type of employee on a part-time basis. This category of employee will require special sets of software tools to gain, securely and effectively, the necessary access to library servers or networks, but it may be an option that will enable you to extend the availability of specialized areas of technical support in the library.

Recruiting

The focus of the discussion in this section is on recruiting qualified people into existing library systems positions. Finding the right person for a specific job is always the biggest challenge while searching to fill any open position. When you write an advertisement for a job, include all of the desirable abilities of the person you are seeking, but keep in mind that few candidates will possess the entire range of qualifications as described in position announcements (Chu, 1990). In terms of systems positions, a key reason for this is the rate at which the technological environment changes. When recruiting, look for applicants who consider themselves change agents or individuals who view new technologies as an opportunity for growth. Such a candidate is more likely to help facilitate inevitable and necessary changes, across the organization and over time, than to resist them. When recruiting personnel, Rowe (in Miller, 1989) notes the importance of change within the guidelines he provides: clarify your mission, look for people who will embrace change, choose labels carefully, involve your leadership team, create paths of opportunity, build in lifelong learning, and require the best (p. 105). Tennant (1998) considers staff hiring to be the most important decision a manager can make because; no matter how technology changes, personnel are likely to remain the same over a sustained period of time (p. 102). He recommends hiring systems staff on character traits rather basing the decision on skill sets (e.g., Perl programming). A laundry list of these character traits includes:

- The capacity to learn constantly and quickly

- Flexibility

- An innate skepticism

- A propensity to take risks

- An abiding public service perspective

- An appreciation of what others bring to the effort and an ability to work with them effectively

- Skill at enabling and fostering change

- The capacity and desire to work independently

More than thirty years ago, in a discussion of the personnel aspects of library automation, Weber (1971) said that it would be "sheer folly" for librarians to try to address every aspect of library automation themselves (p. 29). Seek to hire new staff members whose traits complement those working within your department instead of trying to find people like the ones you already have. Beyond this, it is important that a new hire have the ability to collaborate with colleagues in the library and the larger campus community. In other words, ideal systems staff should have good "people skills" because of this need to communicate with users and colleagues. Volumes have been written about diversity in the workplace. There are very real benefits in hiring from diverse populations, backgrounds, and points of view.

Promoting people from within the organization is a valid option and one method of creating a path of opportunity that will engender a sense of loyalty and fulfillment in employees. This strategy is often employed in libraries. Epstein and Freeman (1991) found that 80 percent of system administrators had held positions ranging from clerk to director within the same library. Recruiting within the library can eliminate the need for a new hire to learn how the organization works. It also may reduce training time because a qualified candidate likely already understands local policies and procedures.

The rest of the world also affects your ability to recruit. During the dot-com boom of the late 1990s, systems librarians were often recruited by the corporate world. This has lessened somewhat, but pay close attention to the broader information technology job marketplace while recruiting. This holds especially true for IT staff positions. It is often difficult to locate IT professionals with skills specific to the library computing environment. When searching for staff positions, look for individuals with a strong understanding of basic IT skills (i.e., operating systems, productivity software, networking) and the ability to learn the specifics of library computing (i.e., ILS management, library specific software, etc.). A service orientation is also a trait that others in the library will expect of IT professionals. As difficult as it might be to assess a candidate's commitment to service via resumes or applications, you can write interview questions that might give a better indication. For example, write a question that asks the candidate to prioritize three or four problems awaiting resolution. A great deal can be learned about a candidate's service orientation based on how and why certain issues are prioritized.

In addition to skill sets, one of the most commonly overlooked characteristics is an elusive quality that is sometimes called "fit." This refers to the ways in which the candidate may interact with others in the organization, including the supervising librarian. Interview questions that are open may help reveal this quality. Sample interview questions might include the following:

1. What's the greatest asset you'll bring to our organization?

2. What kind of tasks would you rather assign to others?

3. What was your favorite position, and what role did your boss play in making it unique?

4. Tell me about your least favorite position or responsibility.

5. Where do you see yourself in five years?

6. What makes you stand out among your peers?

7. Have you ever offered an idea that reduced your department's operational costs or increased efficiency?

8. What's been your most creative achievement at work?

9. What would your current supervisors say makes you most valuable to them?

10. What are the broad responsibilities of a library systems office?

11. What aspects of your current job do you consider most crucial?

12. How many hours a week do you find it necessary to work to get your job done?

13. How do you think your position relates to the overall goals of the university?

Large organizations are likely to have a personnel office to assist in recruiting. Campus or governmental policies might also be in force. If the library doesn't have a recruiting handbook or staff, you may also wish to consult Kathleen Low's 1999 book, *Recruiting Library Staff: A How-To-Do-It Manual for Librarians.*

Job Descriptions and Performance Reviews

Keeping accurate job descriptions is beneficial for a number of reasons. For instance, advertisements can be placed for an opening more quickly when a current, accurate, and complete job description is available for every position. This means that valuable time isn't wasted developing language while a position remains unfilled. The person in each job knows that job better than anyone else and should be the person responsible for a regular review of their job description, especially during periods of rapid technological change.

Many libraries operate under the constraints of civil service job titles, categories, and descriptions. Under those circumstances, job descriptions tend to be general, intended as an umbrella for all jobs in a category, but the actual work done by the people in those categories can vary widely. Not every line in every job description needs to be unique. De Klerk and Euster (1989) encourage a measure of redundancy and overlapping responsibilities because they reduce the risk of lapses in service and introduce organizational change gradually (p. 467).

It is important to be specific, however. Although it is often used to indicate a supervisor's role in establishing priorities and making assignments and is often required for legal purposes, try to avoid the catchall category "Other Duties as Assigned" as a major element. The more specific the job description is, the better the person in that position will understand what the supervisor's expectations are. "Customizing the description of . . . work both will help us achieve the required results and will also serve to challenge the abilities of the particular person who is holding the job" (Trotta, 1995, pp. 47–48). Keeping a job challenging is another reason to review each job description regularly. A form you can use to develop job descriptions is included in the "Resource Materials" section at the end of this book.

When expectations and challenges are specific, it is much easier to make an honest evaluation appraisal. "Performance appraisals are necessary on an annual basis, and they are best when they are developed in collaborative planning sessions between the supervisors and employees" (Trotta, 1995, p. 89). Many organizations will have performance appraisal processes in effect, and the systems office is likely to follow these and adapt them for specific skills and positions. Ideally, planning evaluation criteria is an ongoing process of negotiation, not a once-a-year event. Regular coaching and communication makes the entire performance evaluation process much easier for both supervisor and employee. A valid approach to performance appraisal is to begin with the formal job description and develop quantifiable goals for each essential area of responsibility. Establish personal goals and make them quantifiable as well. Quantifiable goals resemble quotas in a certain sense; they can be met, exceeded, or not met. If the targets are realistic, evaluation will be fair. An example of a quantifiable goal might be the following: Can install the operating system on a workstation within one working day. A sample performance evaluation form is included in the "Resource Materials" section at the end of the book, or you may wish to consult http://www.librarysupportstaff.com/jobdescriptions.html.

3

Communication

The need for excellent communication is recurrent in library literature and position descriptions. Foote (1997) found the ability to communicate effectively among the most critical skills, being explicitly
required in 57.4 percent of the position announcements she analyzed (p.
522). There is absolute agreement in this area; there is no quarter for the
shy, silent hermit devoted exclusively to library automation. In a digital
environment, communication increases in importance because it represents "a shift from a tangible to an abstract environment" (Hoffmann,
1991, p. 55). Parkhurst (1990) offers, "a systems librarian has to deal as
much with people as with machines, and must have good communication skills combined with patience, tact, and understanding" (p. 96). In
nearly all reports, a perception exists that communication within the organization could be greatly enhanced.

Information technology can be used across the organization as a
tool to "shift the emphasis from control of information to sharing it"
(Connell & Franklin, 1994, p. 613). Strategies for improving organizational communication include raising the knowledge level of all staff
members; convening ad hoc, topical cross-team or interdepartmental
meetings; advocating cross-training; and writing memos or articles for
distribution via e-mail, intranets, or internal newsletters. Muirhead (1994)
surveyed systems librarians to determine their primary sources of information. His results indicate that face-to-face communication with peers
outside of the home organization is valued the highest (p. 16). Communication with peers via e-mail and listservs is also a powerful tool.

Like every other culture, libraries have a secret language or jargon that can inhibit clear communication. Those with a background in library instruction are usually aware of this and strive to define unfamiliar terms clearly. Systems people are especially susceptible to the pitfalls of jargon and need to articulate, define, or avoid unfamiliar terminology to improve communication. The systems librarian and IT staff need to be aware of this. Encourage staff to think before speaking or writing on technical topics. In many ways, the systems staff serves as technology translators. An important trait of seasoned library staff is the ability to clearly explain highly technical topics in layperson's terms to nontechnical colleagues. The use of jargon might lead to a perception of secretiveness, which in turn leads to unnecessary conflict.

If conflict develops, do not let it escalate. Try this: Schedule individual meetings with key people involved to plan and establish common technology-centered goals. Seek input from your library director. Avoid the temptation to recruit allies and demarcate "sides" in a conflict situation.

Several authors have commented on the role of communication in the library workplace. Rumors will be the result if the facts are not clearly and completely communicated to the entire library staff. Employees do want to know what is happening in terms of technology. What might seem like over-communication to the systems office might in fact be the exact amount of information that is needed by general staff. It is usually better to communicate technology issues to all staff members even if it seems as if they might not be involved in a specific topic. Staff members who are involved in the early stages are likely to be a good basis of support for technology-related projects (Lavagnino, 1998). Huston and Grahn (1991) emphasize the need to actively involve individuals in order for organizations to adopt innovations. All library employees need computers and technology for a significant part of their daily responsibilities. If they do not understand the nature of computer problems, they will tend to become frustrated. This may lead to unnecessary and avoidable tension in the workplace. One of the crucial communication tasks for systems staff is to communicate enough information to reduce frustration levels. The systems office might choose to sponsor or participate in training sessions to increase the ability of employees to solve their own problems. Chapter 7, "Training," offers more detail on ways to approach this task.

Communication with patrons might not be an activity that would occur to most systems staff, but Corbly (1997) recommends that network managers spend a few hours each week working with library patrons in the reference area to get a firsthand view of the joys and frustrations that users encounter (p. 196). The specifics of this kind of collaboration would need to be discussed in detail with the reference desk staff so that the intentions and limitations were made clear, but it would provide an excellent opportunity for systems staff to become more informed about emerging developments, particularly electronic resources. Cultivating and encouraging an insider's perspective can go a long way toward encouraging smart design of IT systems and services originating from the systems office. Tips for handling complaints include the following: listen, restate what the other person has said to you, explain the relevant policy, offer a positive alternative, never lose your temper, try to end on a positive note, and, finally, follow up whenever appropriate. If you decide to try this approach, avoid defending the status quo; keep an open mind. Take every opportunity to be an active patron of your library's public technology. This will also help you to understand the patron's perspective. You may wish to consult the book written by Catherine Ross and Patricia Dewdney (1998) called *Communicating Professionally: A How-To-Do-It Manual for Librarians.*

Collegiality

Collegiality and consensus are hallmarks of the academic community. These two related concepts make the management role in academic libraries qualitatively different from that in the business sector. Collegiality is characterized by shared responsibility. Consensus implies more than a majority opinion or a top-down decision; it is general agreement. Communication is the cornerstone of consensus building. When you hold a minority opinion, it may be possible to persuade people that your position is the best. Do this by developing a strong body of evidence instead of offering your anecdotal observations. Take the time to research existing literature that defends your opinion. Match the goals you support to the published goals and mission of your organization. Invite guest experts when appropriate; your faculty can be a resource in some situations. Make time to talk to your colleagues individually so that you can be sure they fully understand your position. You can learn to be persuasive—take a course!

Systems staff may have an especially difficult time adapting to the collegial environment for a number of reasons. Because conventional computing education has traditionally prepared students for work in the private sector, employees may have learned to expect that decisions will be made at the top of the organization and handed down to them. Also, those who gravitate toward systems work tend to spend a great deal of time working on problem resolution individually. If you manage a larger department that includes staff with this kind of training or inclination, they may view you as ineffective if your preferred style is to cultivate consensus and collegiality. You will be faced with a set of decisions about what kind of management approach will be most effective under these circumstances. Communicating your expectations clearly and articulating the goals of the department regularly will both go a long way toward avoiding misunderstandings. Make sure your expectations are incorporated into every job description and evaluation process. Refer to the section on job descriptions and performance reviews for help with this. Develop and maintain a clear vision of your leadership role in a collegial work environment.

Every organization is different. As systems librarian, it is important to maintain strong collegial relationships with fellow managers. Understanding the specific needs of library units and departments is essential. This can be accomplished in a variety of ways. Many libraries have regularly scheduled meetings of department heads. It will be of benefit to the systems librarian to have a presence at these meetings, even if irregularly. It could also be useful to have one-on-one meetings with manager colleagues to share information.

Electronic mail has created new channels of communication. In large, decentralized libraries, the use of e-mail might have the side effect of reducing in-person contact. Visit remote departments on a regular or semiregular basis. Even a quick visit will indicate to the manager and staff of that location that the systems office is involved and aware.

Supporting Library Patrons

Library staff is generally the primary clientele for systems offices. Most systems offices also provide some support for library patrons or users even if it is indirect or minimal. What does it mean for systems offices to support library users? For the library systems office, support dictates a primary focus on computer access to library resources. This usually means maintaining public access workstations. Librarians who have a background in working at the reference desk are frequently dedicated to filling the information needs of their public. Systems staff members with reference experience have little difficulty in transferring this kind of dedication to meeting the needs of people who need to first understand how to use the required tools to find the information they need. There will always be a segment of the population with specific information needs, but little expertise in the tools that have become indispensable to information retrieval. Those in a systems role are obligated to bridge this gap if they are to fulfill the mission of their organizations.

Systems staff might work with public services colleagues to seek informal opportunities to work with students or faculty at computer stations. This is an excellent way to gain knowledge about whether the tools you are providing are meeting people's needs. It is nearly inevitable that you'll be able to teach them something that will improve the results they retrieve. Doing a task for others instead of teaching them how to do that task it is an easy trap to fall into. More formal options for teaching include offering orientation classes, writing instruction brochures, integrating instructional materials into Web sites, and publishing periodic publicity announcements or tips in campus newspapers or other publications. In a university setting, 25 percent of the student population changes every year. It may seem obvious, but each new group needs the benefit of the same information you may have shared the year before. Don't assume that sharing or publicizing something once will have an effect that carries over into subsequent years. This is particularly true given the rapid rate of change in the arena of electronic resources and services.

Depending on the library's organization, remote users are a growing population that some systems staff will support. Sometimes this responsibility falls to public services staff, and systems is called in for difficult problems. Communication with this group is done largely over the telephone or electronic mail. Questions from remote users may sometimes cluster around what might be new features or services. Identify this clustering from careful logs of incoming questions. If calls start to seem repetitive, consider developing a checklist for support staff to ask in providing assistance. This will help provide a level of quality control and ensure concise responses. Incorporate responses to commonly requested information into the library's Web page FAQs (frequently asked questions) whenever it is feasible in your situation. These documents can then be easily forwarded in response to e-mail questions instead of having to recompose the answer each time an e-mail question is received. More information about the mechanics of a help desk can be found in Chapter 5.

Professional Reading

Professional reading is one of the most useful ways to stay current in librarianship and current technology. This activity is a useful way to learn what peer institutions are doing about common problems or issues. Think of professional reading not only as a method of staying current, but also as a way to stimulate new approaches to existing tasks, projects, or problems. You can find a number of title suggestions for your reading list in "Resource Materials" at the end of the book. Personal expense can be minimized if your serials department makes routing copies available. Routing is effective when each person on the routing list forwards issues along promptly, but that may not always be the case. Some library system vendors support e-mail notification when a periodical issue is checked into the library. Kohl (1995) mentions UnCover Reveal (now Ingenta) as a popular method to have the table of contents sent to your mailbox for titles such as *Library Journal* or *Library Hi Tech*. Sometimes services of this nature have been referred to as selective dissemination of information (SDI). Reveal allows each subscriber to select up to one hundred titles from their service. This makes it easier to scan article titles that may be of interest to you rather than waiting for a routing copy to arrive at your desk. You can visit the Ingenta Web site (http://www.ingenta.com) for more information about this service. Many other electronic journals offer notification services of their own. Check the journal's Web site or subscription policies to see whether they offer added features.

Some journals are sent as a benefit of professional memberships, for example, *Information Technology and Libraries (ITAL)*, which is sent to members of the American Library Association's (ALA) Library and Information Technology Association. If you find that the journals you receive with your professional memberships aren't relevant, consider the possibility that you might not be affiliated with the appropriate professional organization. Keep in mind that the journals you receive as part of memberships probably are insufficient to support all of your research and educational needs.

Some library journals, like *LJ Online*, are available in electronic formats, either directly from the publisher or through aggregator services. Increasingly, libraries have large numbers of online subscriptions available, at least for the current issues. Because we are talking about current awareness here, the lack of retrospective issues shouldn't be a problem. Identify titles that are most useful and then put a tickler into your personal calendar when you expect a new issue to be published. Access is most convenient if your library has a record of these publications in the online catalog that include links to the full text journal.

Research and Scholarship

In academic libraries, research and scholarship are valued, encouraged, and rewarded because these pursuits are the mechanisms that advance learning, the central mission of higher education institutions. Because of this centrality, some level of research and scholarship are usually a component of the annual evaluation process for academic librarians. Some level of publication record may be expected; tenure or promotion in faculty rank may be awarded. These expectations should be explained thoroughly during the interview and hiring process, but assumptions in this area are sometimes made. Be sure to ask questions until there is a clear understanding. There can be an expectation that graduate schools of librarianship will train prospective librarians in theory, research methods, and literature searching. If the curriculum that you experienced was more applied in nature, you may need to gain these skills by another path.

There is no single correct route to a successful research project. Some people struggle to identify a research interest, while some develop an interest early and continue to explore its facets throughout their career. In the discipline of systems librarianship, the number of potential research projects is large and constantly growing. The idea of undertaking research is intimidating to some librarians, but enjoyable and rewarding to others. Some people find research a natural extension of their student experience, but it is a process that can be learned in other ways, too. Collaboration with experienced researchers is one way to gain some experience with a process that might seem obscure to the uninitiated.

When faced with a large-scale project, think of ways to turn the work you have done into a research project. By addressing the issues in such a project, it is likely that you have already completed the groundwork and research for an article, paper, or poster session. The field of librarianship is filled with opportunities for scholarship. Start with a practical topic and develop a poster session or a case study. In certain situations, such preliminary work may be developed into a refereed paper or article.

Contemporary research relies heavily on facility with the Internet, because new and vital information, tools, and products can be distributed most quickly this way. Internet search tools available to researchers today can't be considered exhaustive. *The Invisible Web* (Sherman & Price, 2001) offers practical advice on discovering Web resources that are not easily indexed and retrieved by conventional search engines.

If research is the way knowledge is advanced, the logical outcome of research is to share its results. There are a variety of avenues to accomplish this, including ALA poster sessions, panel presentations, free or paid consulting, state or local association periodicals, Web sites, refereed journals, book chapters, and ERIC (Educational Resources Information Center) documents. Depending on the evaluation criteria in your institution, each of these methods of distributing the results of your research may carry more or less value. The value placed on each of these outlets generally correlates with how rigorously the results are reviewed by colleagues and experts in the field. Junior systems librarians may appreciate mentoring assistance for their research endeavors.

Leadership

In times of rapid change, a leader must possess a vision that anticipates radical transformation. Leadership skills are crucial to the technology manager in a number of situations. For example, you might be tapped to convene a task force to coordinate a technology-related issue. Incorporating some of the following pointers may ease the process. Encourage broad-based participation across departments and levels of staff. Establish predictable meeting schedules. Seek topics from the group for each agenda. If employees feel they have something at stake in a project, they will work hard to see it through. Involvement in the process will clarify the long-term benefits not only to individual participants but to the organization as a whole. The person who suggested the topic should be able to summarize in advance the background and details that make it relevant. Publish and distribute agendas before each meeting along with any background reading so that the group can prepare for discussion. Conduct meetings according to an orderly and predictable method. Encourage everyone to participate in discussions. Some need to be drawn into discussion; others need to be discouraged from monopolizing it. Send out meeting reminders. Distribute timely meeting notes. When committees comprise more than ten people, communication problems tend to develop. Consider dividing a large committee into working groups, if appropriate.

Sweeney (1994) envisions the leader of the post-hierarchical library to be a "planner, coordinator, motivator, negotiator, innovator, communicator, listener, recruiter, risk-taker, problem-solver, and evaluator" (p. 62). The library leader must be "flexible, energetic, empathetic, wise, creative, courageous, principled, gregarious, determined, and possessed of a sense of humor" (p. 83). "Sharing responsibility for the library and at the same time developing self-esteem in others can be done through: delegating, motivating, coordinating, communicating, and instructing" (Walster, 1993, p. 117).

Many resources identify leadership traits. Trotta (1995, p. 54) attaches importance to the following characteristics:

- Action oriented
- Able to set and implement priorities
- Analytical and systematic
- Makes the tough decisions
- Self-confident
- Strong communicator
- Self-controlled
- Can manage groups
- Objective, good listener, and tolerant
- Shows stamina and humor
- Accepts responsibility and is accountable
- Manages time well
- Mentors others

Stress

Sometimes technology alleviates stress; other times, it causes it. More than a decade ago, manual and repetitious tasks were identified as a cause of stress. "The workload of the information service was reaching such a degree that each member of the staff was overstressed and all library functions were suffering" (Myllis, 1990, p. 29). Now, after years of striving to automate staff workflow, systems people sometimes feel that they have two modes of operation: damage control and disaster recovery. Some days all human contact is the result of a problem or a complaint. Stresses can quickly accumulate and seem overwhelming. "Stress is becoming a serious threat as libraries become more automated and pressured to provide instant services with reduced staffing levels" (Morris & Dyer, 1998, p. 77). Some blame change for stress, especially when it is associated with technology, but change is not a discreet event. It is a process. As a process, it demands input and participation by all stakeholders. In Muirhead's 1991 survey, respondents found that technical knowledge and training help reduce stress (p. 20). Managers should delegate work when possible. Employ cross-training so that several staff members can share tasks. White (1990) recommends that there should be at least two staff members on hand who are capable of making a decision if trouble arises (p. 259). Stress can result in lowered self-esteem and a demoralized staff. Walster (1993, p. 110) offers some suggestions that may help reduce stress levels:

- Think about your accomplishments using positive labels.
- Agree with compliments offered and keep them in mind.
- Reinforce positive comments with action.
- Keep a written file of compliments.
- Recognize the accomplishments of others and compliment them.
- Use visual imagery as reinforcement.

Think of the office environments typical of the dot-com companies in the 1990s. Foosball tables, fish tanks, and video games were commonplace. All of these were efforts to add a little fun to the daily routine and reduce stress at the same time. Stress can be exaggerated by taking things too seriously. It is often difficult to stop in the daily routine, take a breath, and realize that everything really will turn out OK. Rockman (2003) advocates bringing some fun into the workplace. Yes, libraries have a major role in the scope of today's universities, but, as she points out, libraries "are not the Mayo Clinic looking for a cure for cancer" (p. 110). Take a break from the routine even if for just thirty or forty-five minutes a month. Morale could improve, and employees will be reenergized. At a bare minimum, encourage employees to realize the importance of regular breaks and meals.

Laughter helps reduce stress. Clip and tack up a technology-related cartoon if you see one that makes you laugh. Chances are someone else will see the humor and enjoy it, too. Most information technology workers are familiar with the Scott Adams's syndicated cartoon "Dilbert." Bill Barnes and Gene Ambaum publish a comic strip called "Overdue" that is set in a library (http://www. overduemedia.com). It's become so popular that their Web site now offers several strip-related items for purchase. They've even exhibited at the ALA conference. Under appropriate circumstances, it can help reduce stress if we can step back and laugh at ourselves.

Interorganizational Relationships

No library systems office is an island complete unto itself. It exists in relation to other library and campus departments. To function effectively, it is important to realize the depth and complexity of these relationships. We have chosen to highlight a selected number of relationships with stakeholders, national organizations, and vendors. Your relationships will be as unique as your office.

Stakeholders

Spend some time identifying your stakeholders. In an academic setting, they generally include faculty, staff, and students, but, like the ripple in a pond, the ever-widening circle can affect the campus computing center, research centers and institutes on campus, consortia, state libraries, sister institutions, and state and national associations. Foote (1997) found that "slightly over two-thirds of the [job] announcements request that the systems librarian serve as the library liaison to the campus computing center, automation vendors . . . academic departments on campus, professional organizations, and bibliographic utilities such as OCLC [Online Computer Libraries Center]" (p. 521). Each task undertaken may have a unique subset of these stakeholders and others as well. One of the most vital stakeholders is the chief library administrator. Without the support of this key individual, the needs, visions, and projects of the systems office are not likely to meet with much or any success. One of the roles of the chief library administrator is advocacy on behalf of the library in interactions with the provost, deans, and members of the academic faculty.

In the past, the integrated library system was the primary service supported by systems offices. Today, however, the ILS is only one component of an entire range of library information services. The systems office will play a key role in ensuring that all library services are integrated into the larger campus environment. Campus computing centers represent resources and expertise the library needs for peak performance. In some cases, the computing center negotiates selected productivity software licenses for the whole campus. To remain in compliance with licensing agreements, the library systems office must be cognizant of the outcome of these negotiations, which are subject to change from year to year. Mergers between libraries and campus computing centers have sometimes been successful, but especially when the units are separate, regular contact and communication are indispensable. Periodic meetings between key individuals can be a good way to share information. Mailing lists for the distribution and sharing of technical information are beneficial, too.

To leverage progress in technology and purchasing power, many libraries maintain an association with one or more consortia. The 1970s witnessed a large growth in consortia that correlates directly with the movement to automate library catalogs (Imhoff, 1996). Hatcher (1995) found significant changes in systems librarians' positions because of the impact of consortial membership. Examples of consortia include the Colorado Alliance of Research Libraries, OhioNet, CAPCON, Washington Research Libraries Consortium (WRLC), Federal Library and Information Network (FEDLINK), Illinois Library Computer Systems Organization (ILCSO), and Michigan Library Consortium (MLC). The focus of each library consortium will depend on the needs of its membership. Some consortia, such as CAPCON, negotiate primarily with one provider, such as OCLC. Especially where electronic resource contracts are concerned, many libraries find it worthwhile to utilize the volume purchasing power of consortia.

As a representative to a consortium, not only will you work on behalf of the library, but you will develop professional relationships with colleagues from other partner institutions. Although the benefits may be indirect at times, this interaction might be one of the most important aspects of consortial membership. Consortia might also provide some shared services to members. For example, a programmer in the consortium office might be available to assist an individual library's systems office with programming needs. Shared technology and infrastructure are emerging issues targeted for discussion within consortia.

National Organizations

The interorganizational relationship between any given library and a national organization can be complex and subtle. Many academic libraries expect, encourage, and reward professional involvement at the national level as the careers of their professional librarians move forward. Some libraries maintain organizational memberships in national organizations. National organizations vary in their stated purpose and in their composition. In certain cases, library membership is based on an institutional profile or a poll by member libraries. Some libraries subsidize national organizations and promote continuing education by supporting the activities and travel of their officers or members. There is a large spectrum of organizations that may exert an interorganizational impact on academic libraries. A sample of these includes the Association of Research Libraries (ARL); OCLC; the American Library Association (ALA); ALA divisions including the Association of College and Research Libraries, the Reference and User Services Association, and the Library and Information Technology Association; the Coalition for Networked Information; Educause; national user groups such as the Innovative User Group; the American Society for Information Science and Technology; and the Internet Engineering Task Force. These agencies may also play a role of legislative advocacy, lobbying on behalf of key technology policy issues. ALA staffs an office in Washington, DC, for this purpose that offers the ALA Washington Office Newsline (ALAWON) to e-mail subscribers. State libraries also facilitate and coordinate communication with their respective legislatures when library interests are at stake. For further discussion of national organizations, refer to Chapter 7, "Training."

Vendors

Another central interorganizational relationship of the academic library is the one between the systems office and the library's integrated library system (ILS) vendor. The ILS vendor provides service and support for the tool that manages all of the materials a library has collected. Although many vendors actively participate in, and sometimes drive, the standards development process, they may still be slow to support standards in every case because it may imply moving away from a proprietary product. They will always tell you that they support the latest technology, but the stability of the deliverables may vary.

Ideally, the ILS software evolves through a process of new releases, upgrades, and new modules. The systems office is the conduit for communication between the vendor and the needs of the library. If this role is neglected, the vendor cannot be expected to understand which new products and support a library really needs. The ILS must be scalable and flexible enough to move beyond simple automation of the old card catalog model and its basic access points. It must also offer ways to integrate new standards and services such as XML and encoded archival description (EAD) capabilities. Integration of full-text, online digital collections compel ILS vendors to be responsive to the changing needs dictated by access to electronic formats. Vendors who don't understand this open the door to lost business. The library will have no other choice than to look for another ILS vendor. This process is called *migration* and is discussed in Chapter 1, "Planning."

Libraries rely on a wide array of vendors that range from book and subscription vendors and publishers, to electronic records, telecommunications, and system vendors. "Vendors are no longer judged solely on their ability to supply books, but also on the added electronic services that libraries believe will make the work of ordering and obtaining books more efficient and cost-effective" (Lancaster & Sandore, 1997, p. 101). Lancaster and Sandore see a shift for vendors from a sales role to a service role. The increase in outsourcing options that vendors provide may be a barometer of this change. Outsourcing arrangements in acquisitions and cataloging shift some of the burden of processing new materials away from the library and onto the vendor before they ever arrive in the building. In the technology arena, computer vendors will often preinstall standard software such as productivity suites, thus transferring some of the configuration work and direct licensing arrangements to the outsourcing vendor. Web-based electronic resources also minimize the work the systems office must do to make them available to users. A certain amount of troubleshooting will always be necessary, such as ensuring installation of appropriate browser versions or IP limiting issues, but a capable vendor can help streamline problem solving by creating a more uniform environment.

Book vendors are intermediaries between publishers and libraries. "What happens to the library of the future will depend to a very large extent on developments in related sectors, most obviously the publishing industry" (Lancaster & Sandore, 1997, p. 84). The shift from print resources to electronic resources is having an impact on the traditional role not only of libraries, but also book vendors and publishers. Lancaster and Sandore suggest that it is advantageous for libraries to be actively involved in this shift, particularly as journal publications move to electronic formats.

An interesting debate centers on what role libraries should assume in electronic publishing. The outcome of this debate will affect the interorganizational relationship between libraries and vendors who provide book and serial subscriptions. Those who advocate for library involvement argue persuasively. The Scholarly Publishing and Academic Resources Coalition (SPARC) is an example of an organization that strongly promotes a proactive role for libraries in the electronic publishing arena. Founded by ARL in 1998, SPARC is an alliance of universities, research libraries, and other organizations acting as a constructive response to problems in the scholarly communication system. SPARC works to create systems to enhance broad and cost-effective access to scholarly information. Nearly three hundred institutions in North America, Europe, Asia, and Australia are SPARC members. There are several obvious technological considerations involved in expanding the role of the library in scholarly publishing. These include preservation and storage, data migration and refreshment, archiving, and access. Graham (1995) predicts that "the ability of the academy to count on the long-term, secure existence of electronic scholarly work will be an important determinant of the success of academic electronic publishing" (p. 332).

Many library consortia build relationships with vendors and publishers through the negotiation of group purchases. Buying in bulk not only reduces costs to individual libraries, but also creates a critical mass of consumers that can influence future e-publishing directions. There are some obvious trade-offs involving local relationships, influence, and control.

There are countless other opportunities to develop relationships with vendors and resellers. Some employ special representatives designated for the educational marketplace. Educational reps often work with other units on campus and may be more cognizant of the rules on your campus, especially with regard to key purchasing and legal requirements.

5

Development

This chapter discusses development in the sense of fundraising for libraries. Fundraising efforts have escalated greatly in the last decade (Jones, 2002). Waning library budgets mean that creative approaches to funding must be thoroughly explored. For example, some libraries may be able to convert operating funds into endowments over time (Graham, 1995, p. 336). Commonly, the library director bears primary, although not necessarily exclusive, responsibility for the financial health of the library. On most campuses, a development office cultivates relationships with alumni and friends with the goal of securing gifts for the university. Increasingly, large academic libraries employ a development professional who coordinates a development effort targeted to library needs. An individual in such a position might monitor grant opportunities as well as assist librarians with grant-writing activities. Many others have active "friends" groups that sponsor a wide range of fundraising activities. Libraries and their parent organizations commonly pursue permanent endowments. Independent agencies are an important resource for funding as well.

It is to the benefit of the systems unit to follow library fundraising work closely because digital resources and the infrastructure required to support them today account for a substantial proportion of the library budget. Funding secured through development efforts is likely to improve the ability to maintain and augment technology initiatives. There may be opportunities to complement development work through the creation of formal project proposals and project plans for technology projects. It's not uncommon for a "friends of the library" organization, where one exists, to sponsor used book sales to raise money on behalf of the library. If permitted by university policies, consider coordinating the sale of outdated equipment with these fundraisers. This kind of project will involve some effort, save the cost of disposal under some circumstances and may actually provide some modest funds for the library.

Marketing and public relations efforts are often targeted to capture the attention of donors. The effort to explain a program concisely to staff, students, faculty, and other members of the university community can be highly rewarding in terms of financial support. Jones (2002), however, cautions that "if an academic library raises a significant sum of money, the college or university may cut funding" (p. 585). The campus may have specific policies governing budget relief and budget enhancing fundraising. It is therefore necessary to understand the campus culture to be sure any fundraising efforts will be of positive benefit to the overall library budget.

It rare cases, an ethical question may arise concerning the expectation of preferential service when a library accepts funding from individual donors. This is in counterpoint to the value of excellent, equitable, and universal service shared by most professional librarians. If libraries employ development specialists, consider whether some kind of buffer might be prudent between funding sources and library employees. "For libraries as a whole, under funding is not a matter of economics, but of values" (Gorman, 1987, p. 152). The dynamic tension between donations and services may be less acute in the context of the systems office than in other areas of the library because financial support generally translates into computer equipment, and machines seldom discriminate among users. Donors might expect access to certain library resources such as electronic materials. Before permitting such access, check license agreements to ensure this meets any explicit guidelines for acceptable use.

Technology Fees

Traditionally, libraries represent an overhead expense funded by their parent organizations because they have no direct income stream from tuition or use fees. Computer centers, on the other hand, may be financed in part through fees charged to students or other campus users. This organizational legacy has not adapted very well to the increasing demand for information technology within libraries. It may be one of the factors that has influenced some universities to merge the library and the computing center in the past. There are other valid reasons to do this, of course. There is a strong argument for including the library in the disbursement of institutionally collected technology fees that may not be obvious to the university business officer. Library management must clearly identify the central role of technology in the delivery of contemporary library services and lobby for an equitable share of these monies.

Some libraries also assess a "library fee." In many libraries, this fee was used in the past to augment the print collection or support services. Even if that was not the case, it may have perceived so by many users. A library fee today might be used to support e-resources or other library technology needs. If such a fee is collected, the library should highlight how it is used to maintain ongoing support in the long run.

Grants

Grant funding can be an important revenue source for libraries. Sources include independently established foundations such as the Mellon Foundation, as well as government agencies, for example, the Institute for Museum and Library Services (IMLS) administers Library Services and Technology Act (LSTA) funds allocated by the federal government, National Science Foundation, and National Endowment for the Humanities. Each of these funding organizations has its own area of interest. For example, the Andrew Carnegie Foundation funded the construction of numerous libraries in the early twentieth century. A related strategy that has been successfully used to develop technology in libraries is to partner with a private business that provides full or partial in-kind contributions. These partnerships are not always an outright gift. They may stipulate certain commercial concessions. Public–private partnerships work best when there are potential benefits for all parties involved. Detailed agreements that outline the roles and responsibilities of all parties are advisable and protect everyone from unwanted liabilities and penalties. Source books for grant identification and writing are numerous. To get started, find a copy of James Swan's 2002 volume, *Fundraising for Libraries: 25 Proven Ways to Get More Money for Your Library* or sign up for a grant-writing workshop. To search for grants, try a search of the Dialog Grants Database (available from Thomson/Dialog, http://www.dialog.com) or look for a current issue of the *Directory of Computer and High Technology Grants* (1991–). Writing grant applications is an invaluable skill that can be developed, but it can be an extremely time-consuming undertaking. Time will also need to be factored for the administration, reporting, and accounting responsibilities when a grant is finally received. Proven grant-writing skill is a qualification frequently included in library management position announcements.

Service and Support

Service and support fall under the rubric of what most academic libraries would consider to be the day-to-day or "librarianship" responsibilities of the systems librarian. The following sections describe not the theoretical, but the actual tasks that the systems professional must attend to during the course of a normal work day. In providing this information, we try to answer the kinds of questions posed by Lavagnino (1998): "When a microcomputer breaks and it is vital to the operation of a library unit, who troubleshoots the problem? If it is broken, who fixes it? If it isn't fixed in the library, who calls a service to fix it, or drives it somewhere to be fixed? How often do breakdowns occur, and how long does it take to get them fixed? How much does all this cost? How much are you paying the person who spends time on all these activities? What other tasks are they not getting done while they perform these systems tasks?" (p. 216). Technology changes rapidly, so there is no way to address every challenge faced by the systems librarian. These sections address the most important issues at the time of this writing and offer strategies for addressing new concerns.

Service Orientation

Creating and motivating a service-oriented team is one of the most important goals that the manager of a library systems office can achieve. Historically, librarianship is a profession rooted in service, and each potential audience—from the library staff, to faculty, to students—expects a consistent caliber of service and support from the systems staff. A job in the library systems office might be the first time some IT professionals have worked in a library or an academic setting of any sort. Systems staff must be made aware of user groups both within the library and among the campus community. Who is the primary clientele? Who is secondary? Explicitly addressing these questions in light of your mission statement may help the staff in prioritizing help requests. The head of the systems office needs to instill a service orientation among all systems staff members. Remind all staff periodically about the importance of service. Encourage them to investigate such as like *Customer Service: A How-To-Do-It Manual for Librarians*, written by Suzanne Walters (1994).

Library staff is a major service-consuming clientele of the systems office. Most library employees take their jobs very seriously and want to know what is going on, particularly in terms of IT. If users constantly ask about problems or make requests for follow-up, it probably isn't nagging but a desire to understand the current status or situation. Thus, the systems office needs to make sure users are satisfied with services offered. One method of building satisfaction among staff is to make "grand rounds," much like an attending physician in a hospital. Visit staff members' desks and ask how their computers are performing. If systems staff recently worked on a reported problem, follow up to make sure the problem was resolved to their satisfaction. If other issues arise during the follow-up interview, make a note and be sure to follow up. If it isn't possible to visit in person, make a phone call. Library staff members depend on their computers to perform their jobs well. Most employees want to do a good job, and computers should not produce an obstacle to that goal. "Poor organizations and demoralized staff cannot deliver good library service" (Gorman, 1987, p. 160).

Because remote access is ubiquitous, library users can be literally anybody and everybody. It is unrealistic to believe that you can serve everyone at the same level, so it is useful to think in terms of levels of service for categories of users. Keep the library's mission and primary user targets in mind when providing services. Library policy must be clearly stated regarding service levels for nonaffiliated or secondary users. Establish consistent communication channels for remote users and for tracking each contact. More specific ideas about ways to accomplish this are presented in the "Help Desk Services" section that follows.

A significant part of the perception of excellent service involves its marketing and promotion. Academic libraries often face a high percentage of employee turnover each year, so the services and support available to employees must be continually promoted (Kalin, 1991, p. 203). After promoting a service to the public, all members of the library staff must be prepared to provide that particular service. Placing users first, or in other words a service orientation, is crucial to the perception that the library is a good one. "Modern conditions dictate that the library provide for the increased expectations of communities of users. [These are] epitomized by the change from a production ethic to a service-oriented and service-consuming ethic" (Gorman, 1987, p. 152).

Help Desk Services

The help desk is one of the key elements in a successful systems organization. It functions as your central contact point for service and assistance. In fact, the help desk service is as significant to the systems organization as the reference/information desk or instructional services are to a public service unit in the library. However this service is designed, whether a physical location or a virtual location, the help desk must facilitate communication with end users. A help desk might be staffed for certain hours of the day, or interactions can be conducted entirely online. The size of your organization and the skill sets of your users will influence the design, features, and services provided by the help desk. Although you can train library staff to recognize common problems and to perform some basic troubleshooting, when a problem cannot be resolved, everyone needs to be familiar with the reporting and escalation procedures. The help desk should provide simple ways of reporting hardware or software problems as well as tools to help users solve problems on their own. An example of a basic reporting form is available in the "Resource Materials" section at the end of the book. Technology has increased productivity in academic libraries, but that benefit comes with growing pains. The help desk must be designed to alleviate this pain. This section describes the variety of help desk functions and applications utilized in academic libraries today and assumes the systems office's primary clientele is library staff.

One challenge in establishing help desk services is determining appropriate staffing levels. This can be complex because any systems organization can expect to support a wide range of problems from a broad community of users. In most library systems offices, it is difficult, if not impossible, to staff a help desk around the clock, but there must be mechanisms for expediting bona fide emergencies. During normal working hours, there should be a personal contact available as consistently as possible, whether via telephone or e-mail. Some organizations typically support off-hours emergency service by the use of pagers and cell phones, or sometimes providing the home phone number of an on-call member of the systems department. One person might be responsible for all of these duties in a small organization, but in a large library, all members of the systems team should play a role in help desk services.

No matter the size of the operation, the way services are delivered is extremely important. Defining the roles of each service point within the library varies from library to library. Kalin's (1991) article on providing support for remote public catalog users, although often the responsibility of the reference department, provides useful advice for technical help desk staffers. She suggests that help desk workers should be friendly and possess good listening skills. They should also have the ability to understand problems from the user's perspective and know how to deal with difficult people. Credibility is also key, so help desk staff must understand the user's expectations, serve as advocates, and be willing to provide alternatives for assistance if the problem is not readily solved (p. 207). Sufficient training and support must be provided to the help desk staff members so they can provide such services in a helpful and practical manner.

After staffing concerns are addressed, the way in which help desk services will be offered must be determined. The help desk will address problems from the straightforward (e.g., "my computer won't turn on" or "my printer doesn't work") to the more complex (e.g., "which formula do I use to find a percentage increase in Excel?"). A centrally organized procedure with a designated source for assistance is desirable not only for the users' benefit but also to make the best use of the help desk staff's time. Integrate efficient problem reporting and tracking strategies into whatever types of services are implemented. The resulting service must be effective for everyone who seeks service from the help desk.

An important step in providing effective support will be to determine what problems the user can or should be able to resolve without intervention by systems staff. Common problems can be addressed with self-service tools such as FAQs or troubleshooting and training handouts. Tools such as these free systems staff from one-on-one consultation and allow them to research more highly technical issues. For example, a help desk Web page might have detailed instructions that guide end users through processes such as changing a password on a given device or network. The needs and size of your clientele will dictate the extent of self-help tools you must provide. Self-help tools will not replace the need for help desk staff. Some users will always need hands-on assistance.

Many useful tools are available to assist in designing visual or interactive help resources. A simple way to make online help pages useful is to include screen shots of what the user might expect to see on the screen. Limited capabilities are typically available in the operating system (via the "Print Screen" key), but inexpensive software tools such as TechSmith's SnagIt (http://www. techsmith.com) might ease the process or provide enhanced capabilities such as freehand capture of any portion of the screen or capturing cascading menus.

Often users will more fully understand a process or procedure if they can see how it works from start to finish. Consider using tools such as Macromedia Flash MX (http://www.macromedia.com) or ViewletBuilder (http://www.qarbon.com) to create brief tutorials or demos of common problems or tasks. Such resources can be available on the help desk Web site to guide users through problems at the time they need them. Tutorials like this might be particularly effective for tasks that a user is expected to perform independently but on an irregular basis. For example, if you require that passwords be changed every six months, this would be an ideal application to remind users how to change operating system or other passwords.

If users can't solve a problem on their own, they need somewhere to turn for help. Thus, the most recognizable (and possibly most often used) component of a help desk is a trouble-reporting mechanism. This element of the service will assist the systems staff in organizing, delegating, and tracking calls in a prompt manner. For a trouble call system to be helpful to both end users and systems staff, the systems staff might have to offer training to end users so they know which details are important to report. This sort of detailed information is absolutely essential for effective problem resolution. The person encountering the problem has the most complete information and is generally the one who reports the issue to the help desk. He or she must know what and how to communicate to maximize the possibility of achieving the correct resolution. If a library is large, it may increase efficiency to route all or some problem reports from staff through a supervisor or another designee instead of having multiple members of a department reporting the same problem. Sometimes this approach can reduce reporting redundancies or even solve problems before ever reporting them to the help desk.

An easy and inexpensive means of establishing a help desk service is e-mail, which is familiar and easy for users to understand. It is also easy to create a Web form that users can fill out and automatically send to the systems office. A single, shared help desk e-mail account can be accessible to all members of a systems organization, but what happens when a user's e-mail isn't working? A telephone-based service can be a backup in this event. The University of Colorado at Boulder Libraries has employed an e-mail-based help desk service for many years. In the early days of this service, the most difficult task was reassuring users that systems staff was monitoring the service. In fact, users would often follow up e-mail trouble reports with a phone call to ensure a problem would be addressed. Over the course of several years, however, users gained confidence that a simple e-mail request was the faster way of requesting help from the systems department. This proves, however, that whether voice or e-mail messaging is used to support a help desk, it is crucial to send an acknowledgment as soon as possible after you receive the report.

Library staff isn't always the help desk's only clientele. For public access workstation problems, it might be necessary to post a message physically on workstations about the problem report, its status, and detailed alternatives for the person trying to find a computer to use. Consider putting a more positive spin on the situation by avoiding common if uninformative phrases such as, "out of order" and "computer is down" and choosing instead to say, "we're working on this problem" or "this workstation will be available again shortly." If you believe the resolution will take a significant amount of time to resolve, it may be best to remove the station to your repair area.

Depending on the resources available in your organization as well as the expertise available among your staff, it might be feasible to develop a more complex system. Some organizations are moving toward enterprise help desk solutions. Systems like this make it simple for end users to submit and track the status of problem calls and also have advanced tracking and notification features to help the systems staff manage calls. Some libraries have developed solutions like this in-house, but this approach may require a significant amount of resources, depending on reports and analysis that may be desirable. Many vendors also offer similar help desk solutions, but some can be expensive and difficult to install. If you lack the expertise to develop your own system and require a complex reporting mechanism is, you might opt for a vendor-supplied solution.

These software products vary widely. The simplest include Symantec's PCAnywhere (http://www.symantec.com/pcanywhere) or Timbuktu (http://www.netopia.com/solutions/callcenter). With this software, you can take control of a user's workstation from a remote location to assist with problem solving. You can also push software or make system modifications from a remote site. This is also possible in a Windows XP active-directory enabled networked environment. Other vendors offer help desk products that integrate call tracking with Web-based support and knowledge management. Some, such as Intuit Information Technology Solutions' Track-It software (http://blueocean.intuit.com) also include modules t o assist with inventory tracking and software license monitoring. Magic Service Desk Enterprise Edition (http:///www.magichelpdesk.com) promotes a complete, Web-based toolkit. These vendor-provided solutions offer great features; however, be prepared to pay based on the size of your organization. Other options include Web Help Desk (http://webhelpdesk.com); RT: Request Tracker (http://www. bestpractical.com/rt), a perl-based open source product (meaning it is free); HEAT (http://www.frontrange.com/heat/); WonderDesk (http:/www.wonderdesk.com); and Liberum Help Desk (http://www.liberum.org, free of charge).

Help desk services must continually evolve to keep pace with technology and the library's clientele. Increasingly, for example, some library help desks are receiving calls from remote users who need assistance with access to library resources. Even if another library department, such as reference, is the first point of contact for these types of calls, the systems office is usually involved for complex problems. Calls such as these are increasingly sophisticated and can be time-consuming. This user population may also have a different set of expectations; a remote user is more likely to expect problem resolution in a single telephone or e-mail contact. Therefore, services should be evaluated frequently. Keep logs to track the types of service calls received and the frequency of requests. These data can then be analyzed to provide better user-targeted services as well as to lobby for additional resources such as more staff positions.

Service Standards and Measures

How can you feel confident that your services are consistent and effective? A key element of providing consistent service is to develop and follow a set of service standards. This can be challenging, but your strategic technology planning should prove a useful starting point. The next step will be to determine how to measure the value gained from the services you offer. In an environment of constant change and high user expectations, standards and measurements can play a key role in maintaining a viable systems operation.

IT service standards need to reflect both what your users need and what you can support. As Lavagnino (1998) points out, your users tend to think that the systems office can support everything (p. 218). Because your office might not be able to do this, create policies that define the scope of your support and what you can reasonably be expected to support. Make sure your scope statement is realistic and that the library administration endorses it. Involve users in the development of service standards to gain their perspective about what is necessary. Users will want to have an approximate idea about the response time they can expect when a piece of hardware or software fails. The standards need to balance the needs of the user with the resources of the IT organization. For example, what is the procedure and who should be the primary contact if a vital workstation fails during hours the systems office is closed?

Most would agree that requests for assistance are heaviest immediately following the introduction of a new system or service but will gradually slow down and stabilize over time. You might promote your service standards initially via e-mail messages when a new service is introduced and then publish that information on an intranet page for future reference. One of the obvious goals a library is likely to articulate is to increase user satisfaction. The systems office should mirror this goal in terms of supporting library users.

Informal feedback, focus groups, or internal user satisfaction studies can be used to evaluate whether you are meeting user satisfaction standards. The systems office might choose to measure its success in supporting library staff. It could also be called on to work with colleagues to address satisfaction among library patrons. There are a variety of tools available to help in a technology assessment. The Progressive Technology Project is a national organization working to increase the use of information technologies in communities traditionally on the have-not side of the "digital divide." Although not a library organization, the Project's "Technology Assessment Guide" is a good assessment tool for beginners to use (http://www.progressivetech.org/Resources/PDF/Assessment%20Handout.pdf). An "Information Technology Access Assessment Checklist" has also been produced by the Library and Information Technology Association (http://www.ala.org/ala/lita/litamembership/litacommittees/techaccesscomm/TA_Checklist.pdf). This tool is a little dated but contains many questions that can help to stimulate the end user to think about the impact of technology. Educause's Center for Applied Research recently published a research bulletin titled Technology Assessment: Making Sure We Get It Right. This document focuses on assessment of technology across the campus but provides some valuable insight and resources for libraries (http://www.educause.edu/asp/doclib/abstract.asp?ID=ERB0221). It may be that no single assessment tool will be perfect for your organization, but a combination of elements from a variety of these tools can create an instrument that can function to assess IT in your organization.

7

Training

Training issues of all varieties are a challenge to any organization. Every institution of higher education explicitly addresses teaching and learning in its mission statement. In academic libraries, we must always keep this mission in mind when considering strategies for staff training as well as continuing professional education. New employees need training to get up to speed in a new job. Long-time employees need training to stay current. All employees need training to keep pace with advances in technology. Many benefits accrue to broadly trained employees that may aid in their promotion and retention. The library systems office plays a vital role in this task. In her study of position announcements for systems librarians, Foote (1997) found that training was listed as a responsibility for 59.8 percent of these jobs (p. 521). This chapter addresses a variety of training options that library systems managers can employ in their organizations. In academic libraries, training for faculty and student populations usually falls under the purview of reference or instruction departments, so that is not be covered here.

Training Approaches

Everything the systems office communicates to users could theoretically fall under the heading of training, either directly or indirectly. Teaching and learning theories have long advocated that the most effective instruction is provided in the context of specific tasks. Training facilitates the appropriate utilization of the available technologies (White, 1990). When a member of the systems staff responds in person to a request for assistance, urge that staff member to explore that one-on-one contact as a training opportunity. Encourage the requestor to take written notes for future reference. The systems staff member should ask questions to ensure users really understand the process or procedure they just learned about.

The systems office has a dual responsibility for both the training of its own personnel and those outside the office, that is, the library staff. Effective training is one means of increasing staff satisfaction and reducing staff turnover. Remember that individuals have more than one learning style. Try to vary the learning environments the systems office sponsors. Incorporate the principles of adult learning: relevance and prior experience. Do not overlook opportunities for mentoring. There is also a wide variety of certification programs in the IT arena that some libraries might decide to fund for systems staff.

Within the systems office itself there is usually a natural curiosity and a desire to be involved in learning new technologies. Systems managers should encourage interest in new technologies among the staff. This might help to reduce the possibility that systems staff will feel ignorant when working on a problem. End users expect systems staff to know everything about technology. This can be a good thing or a bad thing. Systems staff members need to know which problems they can resolve immediately and which need extended work. Experimenting with a problem on a user's computer might help with the resolution. Everyone makes mistakes. It's OK for systems staff to admit this and to explain that not every problem has a quick or an easy fix. If systems staff maintain a "know-it-all" attitude, it will be difficult to turn problem resolution into training experiences.

Look for a balance between your educational mission and a realistic assessment of skills that exist within your organization. Recognize deficiencies and encourage ongoing training to address them. Allow an adequate training budget because systems staff training is likely to include outside workshops, travel to vendor-provided training, system-specific certification, or other more prolonged commitments. In 1991, Hoffman found that training costs are typically 1 to 2 percent of the payroll budget, but in the current environment of proliferating new technologies, this percentage is almost certainly a conservative estimate. Because technology training is typically expensive, the training budget for the systems office will likely need to be higher than most departments.

Making training materials available and keeping them current can go a long way toward maximizing the effectiveness of anyone responsible for technology training. Although it may not be feasible to arrange a class when a single person has a training need, that person might be able to gain the information he or she needs from a well-planned, step-by-step handout with appropriate exercises, developed for a previously scheduled class. Some people prefer to learn from written materials, but this option won't be effective for everyone. Neither will training materials be effective if they are obsolete and out-of-date. Someone must take responsibility for archiving obsolete handouts and verifying that those that are available are accurate, up-to-date, and complete.

Wilson (1989) suggests exploring the possibility of creating self-paced instructional materials based on transaction logs. Many systems departments have access to a multitude of server transactions logs; search logs are sometimes available in ILS software. Search errors that appear in these logs can be a useful resource in the identification and correction of software misconceptions. The Macromedia Flash product is one example of software that provides relatively straightforward animation authoring tools that can be used for Web-based tutorials. Consider developing other contemporary training materials such as slides created using presentation software such as Microsoft PowerPoint, World Wide Web programs, or custom CD applications. Decide whether hypertext training materials can be used on both your intranet and the World Wide Web, in other words, for both the public and for staff. As discussed in the help desk section, training materials to supplement one-on-one assistance can be useful tools when published on the systems Web site. Some systems Web sites are only available within the library. However, other systems Web sites are available to all Internet users. See, for example, the Systems Department Web site at the University of Oregon Library (http://libweb.uoregon.edu/systems).

If you choose to develop training materials that require specific software, make sure that software is part of your standard staff workstation configuration and that you own the necessary licenses. Training materials that won't work when software is upgraded to a newer release are useless and should be updated, removed, or archived.

Campus Resources

The campus information technology organization is often a good place to start when searching for training opportunities. These units are typically responsible for the infrastructure of the campus and usually offer general training useful to all members of the campus community. Campus computing resource personnel may be viewed as both colleagues and consultants. In most of these units, however, demand outweighs the services that can be reasonably expected. This means that libraries need to assume more responsibility for the technologies they deploy, integrating campus resources into training whenever possible for new tools to be used effectively. For example, you might be able to rely on the campus organization to provide training for e-mail or calendaring applications if those are supported campuswide, but the campus is probably not capable of providing training in library-specific tools such as OCLC Connexion or integrated system routines.

Some universities have contracted with vendors to provide online, computer-based training (CBT). These types of services can be particularly useful for mainstream applications such as word processing, Web development, or operating system instruction. At the University of Colorado at Boulder, for example, the information technology services unit has a site license for SmartForce training and makes it available to all campus users. Online resources such as this allow users to get the training they need at the time and place they need the training.

Professional Organizations and User Groups

Professional associations and user groups may hold regular meetings to share information. Some prominent national associations that provide useful information for the library systems office manager and staff include: Library and Information Technology Association (LITA, http://www.lita.org), EDUCAUSE (formed by the merger of Educom and CAUSE, http://www.educause.edu), Coalition for Networked Information (CNI, http://www.cni.org), American Society for Information Science & Technology (ASIST, http://www.asis.org), and Association for Computing Machinery (ACM, http://www.acm.org). These associations all have different focuses but are similar in the goal of advancing the use of information technology. All provide some sort of training materials and also serve as advocates and lobbyists for information technology within the higher education community. Monitor the activities of these organizations. Beyond discovering training and educational materials, they might provide insight into the experiences of peer organizations.

The concept of "user groups" was born with technology. User groups are communities of individuals interested in a similar topic usually related to computers or technology. They exist independently or under the auspices of hardware or software manufacturers and vendors. A user group is a place where users can share advice and ideas. Some provide free or low-cost training opportunities. Many of these groups sponsor listservs and Web sites where topical discussions can result in creative answers to difficult problems. They can also act together to suggest improvements and enhancements to the product they are interested in. User groups can be national in focus but you will also find many active local and regional groups. Explore the options available in your area and seek an active role by asking others, visiting vendor Web sites, or searching the Internet.

Professional Education

One of the assumptions of this handbook is that many systems librarians were not fully trained for the position in library school. Some librarians moved into the systems specialty after working for many years in other roles. It is clear that the profession expects systems librarians to have the MLS degree. Foote (1997) found that most (92.6 percent to 100 percent) job ads require either an ALA-accredited MLS, or an MLS or equivalent degree. "There appears to be significant confusion over what every librarian should understand about technology and the specialization and in-depth training needed for those who wish to devote their careers to [systems librarianship]" (Wilson, 1998, p. 54). Most library school students come from humanities and social science backgrounds, which poses a hurdle for the acquisition of what some experts consider remedial or undergraduate-level computer training. They argue that this is remedial study that the student must gain independently and is not within the scope of a graduate degree program. All curricular adjustments in library schools must pass the scrutiny of the ALA's Committee on Accreditation (COA). In the United Kingdom, systems librarians responding to Muirhead's 1991 survey rated library school education low in usefulness, while supplier documentation and on-the-job training were given the highest ratings. Miller (1989) and others have suggested that we need to create more opportunities for apprenticeship (p. 104). "There should be more opportunities to provide internships for new library school graduates" (Dougherty, 1989, p. 111). Internships and apprenticeships are a growing trend in the entire library profession both formally via library schools or informally in libraries via job-share agreements. "There is no evidence that a technical services post is the most common route into a systems post, or even that it is a necessary prerequisite" (Muirhead, 1994, p. 20). Rachel Singer Gordon uses the term *accidental* to describe how many systems librarians found their career.

It appears, however, that library schools are beginning to modify curricula to prepare their students for future systems librarian positions. The top five library schools according to a 1999 *US News and World Report* ranking are University of Illinois at Urbana—Champaign, University of North Carolina—Chapel Hill, Syracuse University, University of Michigan, and University of Pittsburgh (http://www.usnews.com/usnews/edu/grad/rankings/lib/brief/infos_brief.php). A review of the curriculum and tracks at these top professional schools reveals the following trends.

The Graduate School of Library and Information Science at Illinois (http://alexia.lis.uiuc.edu/gslis/degrees/curriculum.html#areas) offers four areas of concentration for those pursuing a masters of science degree: Design and Evaluation of Information Systems and Services, Information Organization and Analysis, Management and Consulting for Information Systems and Services, and Access: People and Collections. By following any one of these tracks, a library school student can take courses that would provide a solid theoretical background in systems librarianship.

A similar scenario exists at the University of North Carolina (http://www.ils.unc.edu/html/2_masters_programs.shtml). A masters of science in information science in the School of Information and Library Science requires one core course in systems analysis. Candidates must also demonstrate computer proficiency based on prior experience or by taking a course called Information Technology Applications. North Carolina also suggests a track of courses in networking and Internet technologies that includes courses such as Internet Applications, Introduction to Local Area Networks, Protocols and Network Management, TCP-IP Networks and Network Programming, Information Security, and Advanced Internet Applications. Students may opt for a masters of science in library science that only requires the computer proficiency.

Syracuse University (http://istweb.syr.edu/academics) offers a range of options. A traditional MLS program is available with three central goals: focus on users, effective management of information and information organizations, and appropriate and effective use of information technologies. A management and policy core course called Survey of Telecommunications and Information Policy is required as part of this program. Similar to the program at North Carolina, students may also work toward a masters of science in telecommunications and network management is available. Among the most forward-looking offerings at Syracuse is a graduate certificate program in information systems and telecommunications management. This program is promoted to librarians who wish to increase their information technology skills. The program is also offered to distance learners. A certificate program like this could be invaluable to the practicing systems librarian who feels the need to brush up on IT skills.

The University of Michigan's School of Information (http://www.si. umich.edu/academics/lis) offers a masters of science in information. Of the five top schools, Michigan appears to offer the most traditional library science degree. Some elective courses are available in information technology (such as Information Architecture), but in general, no track for systems librarians is offered.

Finally, the University of Pittsburgh (http://www.sis.pitt.edu/~lsdept/ programs.htm) offers programs similar to those at North Carolina and Syracuse. Pitt also requires demonstrated computer competency and one core course in information technologies. There is no track or specialization for systems librarianship, but one can follow a track leading to specialization in digital libraries that, today, is another element of systems librarianship that future professionals can expect to encounter in their careers.

How can the graduate school experience become more useful or relevant for aspiring systems librarians? Beyond internship opportunities, it might be useful for systems offices to involve themselves more directly with library school faculty in traditional or distance education programs to encourage development of curriculum in support of systems careers.

Staff Development and Continuing Education

Staff development includes a broad range of programming and activities designed to develop the potential of library employees. New systems and technology demand a commitment to staff training. Methods of training mentioned by Glogoff (1989) include "train-the-trainers," self-paced workbooks, staff manuals, and orientation sessions. In an electronic environment, it becomes crucial that training is "treated not as an event, but rather as a process integral with an employee's job (Kriz & Queijo, 1989, p. 64). Cronin (1989) agrees: "It is also clear that staff training should not end when the system has been implemented. Staff members need continued updating on new system capabilities, as well as a structure to channel questions and suggestions for improvements in system performance" (p. 77).

Libraries must provide significant continuing education for not only professional staff but for paraprofessionals or support staff as well (Dougherty, 1989). The differentiation between staff development programs and continuing education is that staff development programs maximize local expertise and focus on the mission of the local institution, whereas continuing education usually employs outside organizations or institutions. It is imperative that staff development opportunities be extended to all staff members so that everyone moves forward, however incrementally. We "need a greater commitment among many librarians now in the field to learn more about computing so that automation development can co-evolve with general library development" (Nielsen, 1989, p. 110).

Who is responsible for ongoing training within the organization? A task force may be acceptable for a single training event but may not be the best choice overall because it is "inherently task-oriented, and once the task has been completed the individuals involved advance to something new or cease to function as a group" (Wilson, 1989, p. 70). Training must be an ongoing commitment. Therefore, some libraries may choose to designate one staff member to coordinate technology-training activities. This role is often most appropriately assigned to someone in the systems office. The systems librarian often possesses an awareness of local technology implementation plans that helps anticipate training needs. It is beneficial for trainers if they both help to develop the electronic environment and work within it. If a trainer does not have diverse experience across a range of library functions, he or she should seek it out; a global orientation is necessary. This responsibility, however, may come with challenges: priority and funding, timeliness, and unrealistic expectations. The technology trainer must be prepared to meet these challenges. Some libraries follow the model of having a committee that coordinates training. If this is the case, the systems office should lobby to have a representative on this committee to encourage appropriate technology training.

Needs assessments often identify technology among the highest type of continuing education desired, so the systems office should be prepared to actively identify specific needs and to address them in training. "Developing new educational initiatives . . . appears to be the greatest challenge facing those who wish to improve our managerial competence in the automation area" (Miller, 1989, p. 104). Trotta (1995) provides some useful steps for developing a staff-training program. When someone other than an employee's immediate supervisor conducts training, employees can view the experience as a development opportunity instead of a test (Kriz & Queijo, 1989, p. 64). "Four important roles for staff training programs are: to enable library staff to effectively utilize complex automated systems; to help library staff manage continuing, rapid change in automated libraries; to implement a frontline service strategy; and to aid employee recruitment and retention" (Hoffmann, 1991, p. 53).

When you invest the time to plan and schedule training, it will be a big disappointment if nobody comes. Consider using the training inducements available to you. For example, you might be able to offer a small salary increment to student workers after they complete a specified number of training sessions. Include your training expectations in staff performance goals (see sample job evaluation form in "Resource Materials" at the end of the book). Encourage and thank supervisors who send staff to training. Offer refreshments. Try to schedule training during low-conflict times. Ask vendors to supply T-shirts or other trinkets for use as prizes or rewards. Seek out guest speakers to lead training sessions. Publicize, ask for an RSVP, and then send out reminders. Use feedback from training sessions to improve the quality of subsequent offerings.

The systems office might not have sufficient staffing to provide all of the required training. One model that has worked successfully is to train the trainers. Current experts on topics can prepare others to train additional staff. When trainees return to the workplace, the trainees become the trainers. Trotta (1995) and Wilson (1989) both support this model because encouraging staff members to become trainers is among the best ways to master a subject. Just as networks have engendered distributed computing, computing should instigate distributed expertise. Miller (1989) echoes this thought, saying, "We must mainstream knowledge about automation because automation itself is entering the bloodstream of librarianship" (p. 104). Nielsen (1989) concurs, saying that placing responsibility on the systems office alone is a "barrier to innovation" (p. 109). Training methodologies listed by Wilson (1989) include videotapes in conjunction with practice sessions, hands-on training, role-playing, self-paced instructional materials based on transaction logs, discussion forums, lecture, demonstration, mentoring, and informal interactions. More contemporary training media include netMeeting, WebEx online meetings, interactive Flash tutorials, intranet pages, and mini-BlackBoard courses that may incorporate chat rooms and video clips, or interactive CD-ROM.

Not all staff development training involves library-specific applications. In such cases, it isn't necessary to reinvent the wheel. You can save a lot of time and effort by outsourcing in these situations. Working within the university framework offers the advantage of a diverse range of local training resources. Look for opportunities on your campus for training in basic software skills such as word processing or spreadsheets. These might be free training sessions offered by campus IT organization for students, staff, or faculty or could be available for a fee from continuing education efforts based within various departments. Some training might be offered by vendors at no charge with other training provided for a fee. There is also a variety of commercial training vendors. Some, such as New Horizons (http://www.newhorizons.com), have several offices nationwide and offer a wide variety of training opportunities both online and in the classroom. Other vendors are local or regional. You can learn about their offerings through local newspaper or trade publications. Many vendors offer discounts to educational institutions, so outsourcing this training has the potential to be very cost-effective. Also check with the various consortia in which your library holds membership, especially the various regional OCLC consortia. These organizations might provide discounted training from commercial vendors such as those listed earlier. If your university has multiple campuses, you might explore training opportunities at those locations as well.

Some traditional professional development techniques are also useful when it comes to technology. Professional conferences have historically played a large role in the development of service-based professionals such as academic librarians. Attending conferences, following the professional and trade literature, visiting conference exhibits, and generally participating in professional organizations are all prospective continuing education opportunities.

8

Daily and Periodic Operations

Because technology changes so quickly, the daily routine of a library systems office is seldom the same from day to day. One of the keys to smooth operations is a thorough understanding of computer basics. Many mainstream publishers offer a variety of reference tools and guides that cover basic computer skills. Ogg's (1997) *Introduction to the Use of Computers in Libraries* does a good job of translating most of the technical details of computer science into the context of library usage. He provides clear and concise explanations of many commonly used concepts and applications that can be useful to individuals with or without a technical background.

Another important theoretical concept to help guide ongoing operations is the Open Systems Interconnection (OSI) model, which graphically describes the standard for interconnectivity. Modern computer networks are designed in a highly structured way. To reduce their design complexity, most networks are organized as a series of layers, each one built on its predecessor. The elements of this model are shown in Figure 8.1.

OSI Seven-Layer Reference Model

Application—provides common protocols

Presentation—decodes transmission

Session—regulates exchanges and handles synchronization

Transport—maximizes efficiency of end to end movement

Network—moves packets from source to destination

Datalink—error removal between nodes

Physical—transmits raw bits through a channel

Figure 8.1. Open systems interconnection (OSI) reference model.

The OSI Reference Model is based on a proposal developed by the International Standards Organization (ISO). The model is called ISO OSI Reference Model because it deals with connecting open systems—that is, systems that are open for communication with other systems. The OSI model has seven layers (http://www2.rad.com/networks/1994/osi/layers.htm). The principles that were applied to arrive at the seven layers are as follows:

1. A layer should be created where a different level of abstraction is needed.

2. Each layer should perform a well-defined function.

3. The function of each layer should be chosen with an eye toward defining internationally standardized protocols.

4. The layer boundaries should be chosen to minimize the information flow across the interfaces.

5. The number of layers should be large enough that distinct functions need not be thrown together in the same layer out of necessity, and small enough that the architecture does not become unwieldy.

The OSI is a theoretical model to help in operational decision making. For example, in a client/server environment, at what level will the primary processing occur?

The daily and periodic operations of the department might be transparent to end users but are absolutely essential in providing the stable information technology services that they rely on and expect. Dunsire (1994) points out that "downtime is inevitable, downtime is bad" (p. 69), but routine preventative operations can help minimize it. Downtime, whether on a user's individual workstation or on a server that supports a group, costs the organization money and frustrates both the staff and the library public. And, of course, equipment or networks never seem to crash at convenient times. The next section discusses the variety of regular tasks that a systems librarian and staff should consider integrating into operations to minimize downtime.

Prototype, Test, Configure, and Deploy

To optimize the time of the systems office, it is essential to develop a plan for deploying computer hardware throughout the library. Everyone wants the hottest new technology such as flat-panel displays. Swapping out computers and parts takes time and can become a serious drain on systems office resources. Develop a deployment and replacement plan and stick to it. Refer to Chapter 1, "Planning," for some useful deployment guidelines and "Resource Materials" for sample policies and working documents. Computer workstations are subject to a dynamic tension between standardization and user customization. Ideally, the balance of these two forces weighs the ease of deployment and maintenance by systems staff against uniquely performed tasks and individual preferences. Similarity and standardization of base hardware configurations speeds the deployment of new equipment and enables users to assist each other. "Technology sharing is usually more important than specific specialized features of stand-alone systems or software only known by a few" (Sweeney, 1994, p. 90). Allowing staff to change screen colors and layouts provides the flexibility to optimize individual work habits and express individuality. Public workstations, on the other hand, benefit from restrictions to customization that can help preserve library branding efforts and guard against problems individual users can cause for one another. Patrons can become confused if library workstations look or behave differently at every use.

When replacing staff workstations, make certain that all unique data files are preserved, especially network settings, bookmarks, and printer configurations. Observe the necessary considerations required by users with accessibility needs, such as low vision. Sometimes it is convenient to temporarily store workstation files on a network server. If a new workstation's configuration is similar to the old one and files and bookmarks are in the right places, staff members will have less difficulty acclimating to a new computer. Individuals who are comfortable with technology might look forward to a new computer, but IT staff must remember that there are lots of library employees who are not necessarily comfortable with changes in technology even though they use it everyday in the workplace.

One way of easing equipment transition is to involve staff members in the process. Consider developing a checklist that the end user submits to the systems office before receiving a new workstation. A sample checklist is included in "Resource Materials" at the end of this book. A checklist helps guide the IT staff through the installation process and enables staff members to share responsibility for technology through a sense of participation. Although most staff members use similar applications, some may need a set of more specialized ones. A checklist can help to ensure that files aren't lost and that all needed applications are installed. This is also a good opportunity for users to clean up their work space by deleting files they no longer need and moving important files to archival media such as CDs, Zip disks, networked storage, or tape.

Once new workstations arrive in the library, they can be unpacked immediately to save space. Unpacking can be accomplished more quickly when several people work together. It can be an enjoyable event when the workgroup devises a system to organize all the pieces needed to make deployment of new systems proceed smoothly. Packaging takes up lots of space, but some people like to save it in case equipment must be shipped away for repairs. You can avoid the waste or recycle problem if you purchase an on-site service contract from the vendor. Be selective; it's unrealistic to save it all. Sometimes cartons can be recycled on campus if certain guidelines are observed. If you can't recycle, notify library staff that the systems office has a supply of boxes free for the taking. Many individuals are always on the lookout for sturdy boxes for a variety of reasons. The key concern is to keep working spaces free from superfluous materials that could also become hazards in the workplace. If applicable, send in registration and warranty paperwork as soon as possible after receiving new equipment. Add the new equipment to the inventory database promptly. (See "Inventory" later in the chapter for more information on inventory databases.) This is also a good time to affix asset management tags if required by the university. If you implement the user-initiated checklist, these can also be affixed to the new computer to keep the new equipment organized.

Set up one workstation and develop a prototype. In other words, install the standard software needed for the group that is to receive the new workstations and remove any unnecessary or unsupported software. Examples of things you may wish to remove include Internet service provider software or software trials that are shipped on some computers. Try not to leave software on the computers that the systems office cannot support. When configuring the prototype for your network, you can avoid IP address conflicts if you have the option to use DHCP (dynamic host configuration protocol). DHCP assigns an IP (Internet protocol) address to a network device for the duration of the connection only and then releases the address back into a pool of available addresses for subsequent sessions. Once the computer is installed in its permanent location, the network settings can be reconfigured to reflect a static IP if that is what your environment uses. Have several people review the prototype to look for anomalies, omissions, or oversights. If appropriate and time allows, ask staff from the group targeted for the new computers to test the setup as well. When testing is complete, you can make a master image of the prototype workstation and replicate that image for all of them. Selected software for creating master images is covered in the following section on hardware maintenance. Many IT organizations use software such as Norton Ghost Corporate Edition (http://www.symantec.com/sabu/ghost/ghost_personal) to clone and create identical setups on multiple computers. This software simplifies installation and also allows the ability to store an image of the workstation's hard drive, which can be useful if it becomes necessary to restore or rebuild the computer in the future. After installing future software upgrades, be sure to capture a new image of the workstation.

Before you start to deploy, communicate your plans to everyone who will be affected, both supervisors and individuals. You might want to distribute a checklist, or census form (see "Resource Materials" for an example). If using a form, ask to have it returned by a specific date. Try to schedule the actual installations at times that are least disruptive to the work of individuals. For public workstations, review the academic calendar carefully and install at times when public services activities will not be interrupted. There is usually a certain amount of customization necessary during each installation, so allow enough time to sit and talk to each person and respond to their questions and concerns. Avoid making major changes before leaving for the weekend or a vacation. This will minimize the likelihood of an emergency while the systems office is short staffed.

Hardware Maintenance

Recommending or purchasing equipment for the organization is often one of the systems librarian's major roles. It can usually be fun to spend someone else's money. Even though this might seem like an easy task, planning and knowledge are needed to make the best use of the college or university's funds. A comprehensive plan for purchasing and maintaining hardware makes the job of supporting this equipment much easier. The plan should include elements such as standard workstation and a replacement scheme. When estimating the total cost of computer workstation purchases, you should also include hidden costs such as networking, replication software licenses, server client licenses, and the cost of disposal or recycling.

Occasionally, disposal and recycling costs may be recovered or minimized through the reselling of equipment the library can no longer use. Some equipment may have depreciated beyond the point where it is cost-effective to take this approach. Reselling equipment represents a large commitment of time and may not be legal under the guidelines of some institutions. Machines should be restored to reflect only the software that was installed when they were received. All data and licensed software must be removed. Purchasers must be aware that they are receiving items without any expressed or implied warranty and that no service support will be provided. In some states there are procedures in place for the auction of surplus equipment. There are probably legal questions about how proceeds from any sale should be handled. Make sure you are aware of them before proceeding with a resale project.

No matter what the size of your organization, you can increase efficiency if you purchase as many workstations with the same configuration as possible. This helps to simplify the installation process because technicians won't need to worry as much about which machine goes where. Staff will feel more positive and more cooperative when they perceive that distribution of new equipment is fair, efficient, and equitable for everyone. Uniformity also eases maintenance and upgrades, for example, the necessary chips will all be the same when undertaking memory upgrades. Purchasing in bulk may also lead to significant discounts.

When equipment fails, it is always important to repair or replace it as quickly as possible. For many hardware failures, the system warranty will cover the broken part and the manufacturer will likely replace it. Sometimes the troubleshooting, repair, and replacement process takes much longer than expected. To minimize downtime, the systems office might consider purchasing a spare computer when making bulk purchases. This extra machine can be stored and used as a "hot swap" replacement for critical machines that require immediate replacement.

Selecting the correct hardware configuration can be a challenge. Think of what peripherals are needed by all users. If the campus organization has established standards, it is useful to follow those. So, for example, if the campus installs Zip drives or CD writers on all of its workstations, your users might also expect them on library workstations. The price of hardware varies greatly depending on processor, configuration, peripherals, and so on. There are several tools that can help in your decision making process. The Federal Depository Library Program publishes a list of recommended specifications for use in depository libraries (http://www.access.gpo.gov/su_docs/fdlp/computers/rs.html). This thorough guide suggests everything from hard-drive size to peripherals and software. It might not be necessary to meet these requirements but the recommendations can provide a baseline for comparison. Other organizations also offer recommendations. The Colorado State Library (among other state library organizations) publishes a list of "technology standards" twice a year that include hardware specifications (http://www.cde.state.co.us/cdelib/technology/techstan.htm). If you are purchasing server hardware, you might want to consult a resource such as *PC Magazine*'s Server Buying Guide (http://www.pcmag.com/article2/0,4149,487990,00.asp). Most software providers will be very clear about the minimum hardware required to support their products. This can also be a guide in determining server specifications.

More mundane types of maintenance can sometimes extend the usefulness of certain pieces of hardware. Perhaps you can afford to hire part-time student staff to clean public workstations and verify that each is in good working condition. At the same time, they can be checked against the inventory database. Summer might be good time for this kind of project because usage is lower. The appearance of public spaces is improved if computers are moved periodically and the table area beneath is cleaned. A handheld vacuum can be useful for removing dust from inside certain equipment and retrieving lost items from inside keyboards. Cleaning supplies that are safe for monitor screens and keyboards come in handy. Before using any cleaner on computer equipment, though, be sure to read the manufacturer's recommendations and observe all warnings.

Networks are a maintenance area that you cannot afford to overlook. As user expectation for full text and image delivery to the desktop increases, so does the demand for network speed, resiliency, and bandwidth. Switch ports should be optimized and synchronized with Ethernet cards to support the fastest possible exchange of packets across the link. Upgrade switches as necessary to take advantage of the highest rates of data transfer that the campus infrastructure can deliver. There are a large number of protocols required for networking tasks. Some of these, like DNS, SNMP, DHCP, and netBIOS, handle network name resolution and addressing. If you manage a network at this level within the library, review network protocol settings and configurations periodically. It is likely, particularly in large libraries, that the systems department will include a network analyst or other IT professional. Even though the systems librarian might not have primary responsibility for this area, it is a good idea to understand some basic concepts. Most campuses provide a great deal of network support. It's also wise to maintain close working relationships with campus experts because their plans will inevitably have an impact on the library network. A gateway connects your local area network to the larger system of networks known as the Internet, usually via a campus backbone. The gateway should support the fastest possible transfer rates so that it doesn't create a bottleneck on your network. Because they are unique, wireless networking is covered separately in a later section.

Printing Issues

So much for a paperless society! Demand for printers increases in proportion to the number of computers in the library. Although file sharing and other electronic solutions might reduce the need for certain kinds of printing, all users are likely to expect access to a printer. Most users like to have a printer on their own desk but that is not always the most cost-effective printing solution. To minimize costs and IT staff workload as well as meet user expectations, it is practical to combine network and standalone printers in your printing environment. Maintaining supplies of ink and toner cartridges will be more efficient if a set of standard printers is deployed.

A variety of printers might be needed depending of the size, function, and layout of library staff office or work areas. Individual offices in remote locations might require a standalone printer but in a space where a group of people work, network printers are a practical way to deploy printing support. This, of course, needs to be balanced with the work flow in a given area. Specialty printers such as label or barcode printers might also be needed in staff areas. Many specialty printers are marketed to consumers, but take care in selecting such printers for a library environment. Workplace printers will receive much more use than those in a typical home environment. Make sure you have identified a vendor to maintain and service these printers as needed.

Printers in public areas have frequently been the bane of the reference staff's day ever since typing rooms in libraries began to disappear. Early dot-matrix printers made a lot of noise, jammed often, and used lots of heavy tractor-fed paper. Today's networked laser printers are quieter and somewhat less troublesome, but users are prone to print anything and everything, thus consuming inordinate amounts of paper and toner cartridges. Librarians have used a variety of techniques to encourage smart printing and minimize waste. Some libraries have removed printers altogether and encourage users to e-mail or download citations or full-text information. Others have placed printers behind reference or circulation desks and distribute print jobs to users by request. Still other libraries put color paper in their printers assuming patrons won't print as much if their output is on, for example, green paper.

Many libraries today have implemented pay-for-print solutions. Depending on your environment, there are a variety of ways to accomplish this, ranging from collecting nickels and dimes at a service point to installing print management software and print kiosks. Some libraries have established policies that set a threshold for free or subsidized printing to help control costs. If a certain number of free copies is exceeded, a fee is triggered. Many campuses have also developed campuswide solutions to printing. One of the benefits to most printing solutions is the ability to cancel a print job from a control screen or queue if it turns out to be unwanted. If the campus has such a program or is investigating one, the library could likely be a major player. One popular way of managing pay-for-print services is to set up print kiosks. In this model, a user would send a print job to the print kiosk. At the kiosk, the user would select the job to print, pay, and receive his or her printout. Many software solutions support operations such as this including Pharos' Uniprint software (http://www.pharos.com) and GoPrint software (http://www.goprint.com/index.html). Both of these products are used widely among both libraries and other academic IT organizations. They have also been frequent exhibitors at library conferences. Deciding on a product requires a significant amount of decision making depending on such considerations as scale of operations and forms of payment accepted. Many libraries also work with a third-party vendor that supports the print software, servers, and kiosks thus reducing the workload for in-house IT support.

CD-ROM and DVD

CD-ROMs have had an interesting existence in libraries. Throughout the 1990s, they were a mainstay because many online information resources such as indexing and abstracting services and full text data were delivered to libraries on CD-ROM. The U.S. Government Printing Office (GPO) embraced CD-ROM technology, and hundreds of CDs containing government publications and data are still created and shipped to depository libraries on a regular basis. Once they arrived in the library, the systems office usually had the responsibility of installing and maintaining these products on client workstations. Many libraries used equipment such as CD-ROM towers to allow simultaneous use via a network. As the prices of disk storage space dropped in the mid-1990s, many CD towers were superceded by devices that allowed CD-ROMs to be cached to disk. Today, of course, many services that used to be shipped on CD-ROM are now available via the Internet. There is speculation that DVD technology will soon supercede CD-ROMs because they can store significantly more data. The GPO, for example, currently ships a variety of depository items on DVD. As technologies such as writable CD-ROMs, also called CD-RW, have become more mainstreamed, CD-ROM has become more of an archival storage medium. This is true even though CD-ROMs don't yet have a clearly established life expectancy. In some libraries, the systems office still has the responsibility for supporting CD-ROM purchases and subscriptions. There are nearly as many variations of this process as there are CD-ROM titles in existence.

If the systems office is responsible for managing CD-ROMs, close cooperation with the serials or acquisitions processing staff will make the job easier. If the reference or documents departments manage their own CD-ROMs, systems staff may still play a role when the original applications are installed or when hardware is upgraded. Careful record keeping is essential. Records should include information about the number of user licenses, whether new disks supersede or cumulate old ones, where application software can be found, installation instructions, and disposition of old media. Superceded CD-ROMs sometimes reappear as conference room coasters or even holiday tree ornaments.

Installing CD-ROM products on public access workstations can be a challenge. Most CD-ROMs are designed and licensed to be used on a single workstation and may require extra customization time or programming to install within a networked environment. Because most of these products today are popular with specialized audiences, one model is to designate a particular workstation as the CD-ROM station. If you have products that must be networked, there are some vendors that provide solutions. Both Axonix (http://www.axonix.com) and Excel/Meridian Data (http://www.excelmeridian.com) offer various hardware and software solutions that can serve CDs and DVDs. For an excellent overview of CD-ROM options and tips, consult Barclay's (2000) *Managing Public Access Computers*. The systems office should remain up to date on removable storage options such as DVD and CD-ROM and be sure to have the appropriate hardware to read these data. Consider retaining some obsolete hardware to read data from legacy storage devices such as 5¼-inch floppy disks that are no longer in general use. This may not be realistic in the long term unless you are prepared to maintain obsolete equipment. Another crucial option to consider is data migration.

Software Upgrades and Monitoring

After considering hardware upgrades, how do you determine whether and when to upgrade software? Software upgrades include both operating systems and application software, and the relation between the two might influence any decision you make related to upgrade timing. Keep in mind that change can cause increased stress for staff members. On the other hand, a different set of problems can be created for systems staff down the road if there is not a systematic program in place to stay current with software upgrades, especially operating system upgrades. A general rule of thumb suggested by some is to stay within at least two versions of a particular current piece of software. Upgrades might be required more frequently depending on the application or if, for example, a user is collaborating with someone else using a newer software release. Corbly (1997) offers the following useful considerations to decide whether it's time for software upgrades:

- The old software supports only a universal printer driver.

- The vendor no longer provides technical support for the version you use.

- Large numbers of macros substitute for software functionality.

- Programmers are no longer writing macros for your version.

- You cannot share data files with other applications.

- Current software will not run on your new hardware.

- A new operating system will not run the older version.

- A newer version receives favorable in-depth reviews.

- Colleagues are using new software successfully.

Browsers are currently the single most popular way to integrate library resources on the desktop and include Netscape, Internet Explorer, Mozilla, Mosaic, Lynx, and the proprietary browser, Opera. Internet Explorer and Netscape currently hold the vast majority of the market share. Plug-ins or helper applications extend browser functionality, for example, Adobe Acrobat Reader, RealNetwork's RealOne (formerly RealAudio or Real Player), Macromedia's Flash and Shockwave Players, and Nullsoft's Winamp MP3 Player. These programs are often available for free download from the Internet. For examples, see http://home.netscape.com/plugins/index.html. Whenever downloading new software, always copy it into a separate directory (such as a temp directory) and run it through the most up-to-date virus checker you have available.

It is also important to stay current with service packs or patches for operating systems or software. Software developers release these to fix bugs found in their currently released products. Many of the operating systems service packs include vital security patches, so it is important to safeguard your network and resources by installing these patches. The widespread nature of events such as the SoBig! Virus and Blaster worm are solid indication of the importance of virus protection and patch maintenance. If you are troubleshooting software problems and need to call the software manufacturer, one of the first questions you will be asked is whether or not you have installed all current services packs and patches so it is a good habit to get into. For applications, you can usually check the version information using the "About" link found in the Help menu. To determine the service pack level on Microsoft operating systems, right-click on "My Computer," choose "Properties" and then the "General" tab. Windows XP facilitates critical updates via the Windows Update option in Internet Explorer. The systems office will probably want to push out updates to client machines as necessary but Windows Update is a useful feature for certain user groups, particularly laptop users. Certain software supports automatic updating, but some automatic updates require user participation to complete. This can be complicated on workstation operating systems that require administrator permissions for updates if the regular workstation operator doesn't have the necessary permissions.

Virus software should also be installed on every server and workstation and kept current by installing new virus definitions as they become available. Refer to "Security" later in the chapter for additional information about virus protection software.

The systems office may wish to employ methods that allow remote viewing of workstation drives and processes. Some are network utilities and some utilize server operating systems. Some utilities also provide a method for updating software and system drivers over the network. If there are a large number of devices attached to your network, this is worth looking into because it may be a way to keep service disruptions to a minimum.

The systems office should consider developing a list of supported software. Such a policy will provide consistency across the organization as well as clarify support responsibilities. The list should be based on a variety of sources to meet all of the software needs of the library. For example, the campus IT organization might have a list of software that it supports. The library's supported software list should mirror this to allow for consistency across the campus. ILS or other vendors might also specify certain supported software. A sample policy on supported software is available in "Resource Materials" at the end of this book.

License Control

License agreements govern most software purchase and use. Enforcing the observance of these may be the responsibility of the systems office. In general, a software purchase doesn't mean you own the code; rather, it means you are purchasing the right to use the software package. Scrutinize software licenses carefully because they represent potential legal liability. Training can help you understand your responsibility. The ARL is one of the agencies that offer programs in this area. Unfortunately, the details of license agreements are as different as the variety of software in the marketplace. Software license compliance is no easy task to manage. Software developers are increasingly conducting campus audits to ensure compliance with license agreements. Software audits protect the organization from potentially costly legal battles, but also protect the rights of the software developer. Read license agreements carefully before copying, providing network or remote access, or installing software on more than one standalone workstation. An even more proactive approach is to negotiate your specific licensing needs with the vendor before the purchase. You do not have to accept the standard license a vendor provides. Determine who, if anyone, on your campus needs to review any legally binding license agreements.

A simple way to monitor conformance with license agreements is to establish a database that lists software titles, version or release information, numbers of users, access method (standalone or network), vendor and technical contacts, costs, and renewal or upgrade procedures. Such a system also provides useful information when purchasing additional licenses or upgrades. Think about categories of information to include in the database. For example, does your license allow for reserve materials or interlibrary lending? Which populations represent licensed users? Are there explicit restrictions on use?

For large organizations, license monitoring can be an especially daunting task. In these environments, it might be useful to investigate automated tools to assist in monitoring. One example of such a tool is Layton Technology's AuditWizard (http://www.laytontechnology.com). AuditWizard can be deployed over the network to gather information about software on remote workstations. Reports can be generated with details about what software is installed as well as version numbers. This tool can also provide you with detailed information about specific pieces of hardware such as hardware or machine (MAC) address and amount of memory.

Many users think of their in-library workstation as their own personal computer. This leads some users to believe they may install applications that might not be licensed appropriately. You can exert some control over this liability by setting group policies that disallow users from making modifications to workstations. If users are allowed to add software to workstations, one way to control this is to create and enforce a policy covering what software a user may install on library equipment. Some libraries allow users to install personally owned software but only if they notify the systems office and sign a form stating that they own a license. See "Resource Materials" for an example. This isn't a foolproof method because it prevents users from installing certain automatic updates, but it should be evaluated as an option. If unauthorized software is a problem in the organization, the systems office might consider installing software such as the AlertMonitor feature available as part of AuditWizard. This software will alert the systems office whenever new software is added to designated workstations.

Server Management

The more you learn about managing servers, the more productive and reliable their performance will be. The utilization of servers varies greatly across libraries. In some environments, the servers you use may be located outside the building. Some libraries operate numerous in-house servers dedicated to specific services, for example, ILS servers, image servers, staff file and application servers, network controllers, and Web servers. This section offers some insight and guidance for those managing or considering internal library servers.

If you are considering the purchase of a server, you will first want to develop a clear idea of its purpose. Talk to experts on campus about their experiences. Ask your purchasing office about recent server acquisitions on campus. Contact the educational representatives of major computer brands such as Dell or Sun for advice about how their products might match your needs. Some vendors provide special Web sites for educational clients to configure and price hardware. If the room in which you plan to house the server is not equipped with an emergency generator system, include an uninterruptible power supply (UPS) of appropriate capacity in the server specification. Consider how your choice of operating system or platform will conform to the existing structure and expertise available within your campus network. Some server components are "hot swappable." In other words, you can replace these elements in ways that reduce or eliminate major service outages. RAID (redundant array of independent disks) disk solutions have gained popular acceptance as a method of reducing server downtime because of the way they employ redundancy to recreate lost data when some portion of a disk array fails. At least two disk drives are required to install a RAID failure. If one of the drives fails, the second can operate the server until the first is replaced. Many server components anticipate the need for expansion capability, but it can be difficult to anticipate how quickly demand for server resources will grow. Remember to include all servers in your permanent equipment rotation plans. Keep in mind that servers might have a longer life span than conventional workstations. Return all hardware registration and warranty materials. Add the servers to your inventory database. You will also need to decide how much technical support you want from the vendor. Keep track of the applicable service contract renewal periods and budget for them.

Managing a server represents a larger investment of staff time and attention than you might anticipate. Hire someone with a specialty in system administration if possible. If hiring an additional position to serve as system administrator is not an option, you will need to develop expertise among existing staff. This may mean eliminating or reallocating other work assignments. Be sure your server budget includes money for server management training. There are many formal training options available from vendors, third-party training organizations, user groups, campus courses, and professional organizations. There are also informal training opportunities available. O'Reilly Media (http://www.oreilly.com) is an excellent and well-established publisher of books related to

nearly every aspect of system administration. You may find it worthwhile to be added to their catalog mailing list or visit their Web site to see the wide variety of computer-related books currently in print.

For the sake of system security, it's important to monitor the availability of any software patches and updates associated with the server operating system. The system administrator will be able to automate partially the installation of certain updates and patches, but most will require the reboot of the server to take effect. Identify low-use periods for each type of server so that a reboot causes as brief a disruption to service as possible. Warn users ahead of time when you anticipate a service outage and provide an estimate of its duration. Watch the trade journals. When you notice coverage increasing for a new server operating system release, determine how long you can safely continue using your current software. Find out when the vendor plans to terminate its support of the product. The consequences of continuing to use unsupported software can be undesirable for the same reasons discussed in the Software Upgrades and Monitoring section. Be sure to keep virus software current on every server, too.

Managing user accounts is a primary concern for system administrators. Keeping user accounts secure is one of the best ways to prevent unauthorized access to your server. Unauthorized access makes the server susceptible to malicious destruction of the data stored there. "One of the main problems of maintaining the integrity of a library database is that of security" (Boss, 1997, p. 50). If you allow users to select their own passwords, they should be educated about how to choose one that is "strong"—a password that includes a combination of upper and lower case letters, numbers, or other nonalphanumeric characters. Consider assigning user passwords using random password generator software. For example, the CertTest Training Center offers a free, online password generator at http://www.certtest.com/passgen.html. Several similar free services are available online in an effort to promote stronger computer passwording. To increase security, the administrator can set passwords to expire after a specified period of time. Users then must change their passwords before the expiration date to log in to the server. Grant permissions to users based on only the resources that they need. There is a delicate balance between empowerment and control when establishing permissions. Most server managers err on the conservative side for the sake of system security. Create groups for users that require access to the same resources. Groups increase administrative efficiency. When changes are required, you will only need to make them once instead of for every affected user account. Be sure to disable accounts when someone leaves library employment. You might also disable accounts after an observed period of inactivity. In addition to keeping your server secure, these measures are useful for keeping within the license limitations associated with your software. Certain licensing agreements for library servers may fall under the umbrella of campus licenses. Some campuses renegotiate their licensing agreements periodically. Establish a channel that will keep you informed of changes in these agreements.

Familiarize yourself with the management utilities available on the server. Supplementary and third-party utilities are often helpful on the server, too. The Windows Resource Kit CDs are an example of a source of supplementary server administration tools. Log files are often a good starting point for identifying and fixing server problems. Explore the toolsets available that can enhance your ability to monitor and manage the remote workstations that are attached to your network. The registry editor and the policy editor are examples of these in the Windows environment.

In libraries that utilize multiple servers, system administrators need to be aware of the distribution of work among them. Review and adjust services periodically to maximize overall performance. Library users should not perceive all of the pieces required for excellent library service as independent, but as a seamless whole. Their judgment and satisfaction will often focus on whatever the weakest piece might be in the complex array of services your servers support.

Data Protection and Backups

Electronic data stored in computer files are among the most valuable assets in your organization. In the event of system failure or a disaster, it is imperative to have backups of important data files. Backups must be done on a regular basis. Different servers may host different types of data. Assess the types of data on various servers and develop a schedule for backups. For example, a mission-critical server such as the integrated library system should probably be backed up daily. Other servers that contain administrative or financial information might also require daily backups. Mail and other file servers should be backed up at least weekly. Consider the implications of privacy in the retention of mail backup media.

Write a formal procedure for server backups. If restoring the system from a backup is ever required, the stress on the system administrator and everyone who relies on server resources can be enormous. It is nearly impossible to anticipate an event of this nature; you can only prepare for it. If feasible, practice your backup and restore procedure before your server goes online. Documentation and familiarity with procedures help minimize panic in the event of disaster. Make careful notes of configuration and network settings, including any services that require a manual restart. You may find it convenient to keep these written records in a binder adjacent to each server. A server configuration reference table can provide a useful descriptive summary. There is an example of a summary table in "Resource Materials." An online file may seem efficient, but it cannot help you if the server is down and you can't get to it.

As libraries build digital collections, backup requirements take on a more mission-critical role. Because true standards are still in the development stages, the data created today might not be readable by hardware or software ten or twenty years from now. This is precisely why the preservation community debates whether items are being digitized for preservation purposes or access purposes. There is a large and growing body of research literature relating to this specialized area of interest, but it is clear that a consistent and systematic plan will soon be needed to provide for future data refreshment and potential migration to different platforms or formats. Although the role of the systems office is still relatively peripheral in this area, there is an apparent opportunity to take a leadership role in the future as libraries focus increasingly on developing and providing access to their digital collections. There is further discussion on this topic in the "Digital Library Initiatives," found in Chapter 10, "Research and New Technologies."

An important element of any backup plan is where the backup media will be stored. Backups should not be stored near the computer where the data came from because there is a high risk that anything causing physical damage to the computer will destroy the backup as well. Ideally, a library should investigate methods of storing backup data offsite. Many a systems librarian has probably toted home backup tapes for storage. This arrangement really isn't ideal, however. A suitable way of dealing with offsite storage is to contract with one of the variety of vendors that offer services of this nature. You can contract with a vendor to pick up your backup tapes and store them in a secure, offsite facility. One of the well-known national providers for this service is Iron Mountain (http://www.ironmountain.com), but you might find local vendors that offer the same services at a more approachable price. A vendor such as this typically picks up tapes on a set schedule. Old tapes are also returned on an established schedule. In case of emergency, the vendor will return your backup tapes or assist with disaster recovery depending on the service level agreement you have established with them. State libraries or archives might also rent archival storage space to public institutions. The cost of offsite data storage might seem unnecessary, yet this is a vital component of a complete disaster recovery plan.

Security

Security encompasses many sets of issues: physical security, network security, and data security. Computer security issues often create dynamic tension against the goal of most academic libraries to facilitate free access to information. It is crucial to achieve the correct balance between these two competing needs. Avoid absolutist thinking. There never will be a completely secure computer. Neither will access to information ever be completely free of obstructions. Both sides of this debate must consider both environment and cost-effectiveness. Security goals and standards should be mutually established, written, and broadly shared. A variety of organizations have publicly posted security guidelines on the Web. These can be useful to review when establishing security guidelines of your own. Try the National Security Agency's Security Recommendation Guides at http://www.nsa.gov/snac/, Microsoft Security Configuration Tool Set at http://www.microsoft.com/windows2000/techinfo/planning/security/secconfsteps.asp, or InfoSysSec's security portal for information system security professionals (http://www.infosyssec.org/infosyssec) for help with evaluating or enhancing the security of your site.

Physical security against theft, vandalism, or accidents might include a careful and complete inventory, locks, alarms, formal checkout control, alert staff, and video camera installation. System security may include a number of software solutions ranging from antivirus updates, filtering, and remote administration to passwords, BIOS, and registry adaptation. The advent of the Windows NT operating system and its heirs added a toolkit for increasing system security. The systems office should thoroughly test any installed security measures before deployment. Maintain a current master image and a boot disk for each type of workstation. It is usually more efficient to rebuild the workstation from a master image than to try to remove or restore individual elements manually. Barclay (2000) lists suggestions for vendors of commercial security software.

Web browsers are susceptible to security problems because they potentially allow anonymous e-mail, customization of user preferences, and access to hard drive files. Netscape provides a stand-alone version that prohibits e-mail and newsgroup access. Carefully consider the impact that disabling e-mail will have for links from Web pages. Microsoft Internet Explorer offers an administration kit http://www.microsoft.com/windows/ieak/en that allows system administrators to disable selected features.

The ALA offers guidance to libraries struggling with decisions about Internet filtering in its "Libraries and the Internet Toolkit." The Children's Internet Protection Act (CIPA) mandates new rules for certain libraries. The toolkit can be found online at http://www.ala.org/alaorg/oif/internettoolkit.html.

Virus and Internet worm attacks have become more common in recent years. They can be accompanied by a proliferation of unfounded rumors and false alarms. The attacks themselves combined with hoaxes create an enormous amount of work for the systems office. Libraries, of course, are not the only entity facing this challenge. Because network access is generally widely available in higher education, the entire university infrastructure might be more susceptible to security threats than a corporate network, which is usually tightly restricted. Thus, network security is a popular topic among IT professionals throughout higher education. Luker and Peterson's (2003) *Computer and Network Security in Higher Education* is a good summary of the current state of security of college and university networks and also includes some sample strategies and policies that might help your library respond to this crucial concern.

The systems department should develop a strategy for dealing with security threats. Advertise virus alerts cautiously and always verify them first with a reputable coordinating agency such as CIAC (Computer Incident Advisory Capability) Security http://www.ciac.org/ciac, the CERT Coordination Center http://www.cert.org, or Microsoft TechNet http://www.microsoft.com/technet. These agencies often provide automatic email alerts, which can greatly expedite the response time of the systems office. Your campus IT organization might also have a security office that provides current information. Many antivirus software vendors publish detailed virus encyclopedias on their Web sites. These resources can be indispensable in preventing damage from virus attacks.

Antivirus software should be installed on all workstations. There is a variety of products available in the commercial marketplace. Many manufacturers ship computers with virus software installed, but when this equipment is deployed, it is important to make sure there is a procedure in place for installing regular updates to the virus definition files. Licenses for antivirus software might be negotiated campus wide, but if not, visit the Web sites of commercial providers to determine the best virus protection package for your environment. Some vendors provide software that helps coordinate virus-fighting efforts across the network. One such vendor is TrendMicro (http://www.trendmicro. com/en/home/us/enterprise.htm). Trend's enterprise software allows systems staff to monitor all computers connected to the network. Many times, viruses can be repaired remotely. This software also allows scheduling of virus scans and pushes new virus definition files out to network workstations when they become available. Other vendors of antivirus software include McAfee's VirusScan (http://www.mcafee.com), Symentec's Norton Antivirus (http://www. symantec.com), and Sophos's Antivirus (http://www.sophos.com). Servers require extra protection from viruses. Panda Software (http://www.pandasoftware. com/products) and other vendors offer server-side virus protection.

You can add a certain measure of security to the computers in your library by applying certain kinds of network software. Firewalls and virtual private networks (VPNs) are two examples of possible network solutions. VPN solutions are particularly popular for remote or wireless network access. The campus computing center may employ an expert in this area. Make contact with that person. If the campus provides firewall services, you might need to negotiate open ports for the library servers. A port that is open across a firewall is sometimes referred to as a "poke" through the firewall. Firewall software is also available for individual workstations and servers. SSL (secure sockets layer) and S-HTTP (secure hypertext transfer protocol) protocols can increase the security for data that are passed between Web servers and clients by encrypting the transmitted text so that it is less easily misused if it is stolen. SSL deployment requires purchase of a certificate from a vendor such as VeriSign or GeoTrust to increase confidence that your Web site is authentic and that all transactions are secured by SSL encryption. Passwords are the first line of the defense of a network. On many systems, accounts can usually be configured to force users to change their passwords periodically. Certain password characteristics can be specified to make passwords more secure as well. Passwords are discussed in more depth in "Server Management" earlier in the chapter and in the sample password policy in "Resource Materials" at the end of the book.

Departmental Procedures

Every library department should have a written procedure manual, but in the systems office, documentation becomes especially crucial. Everyone can tell stories about those mysterious people who can draw every piece of information from memory, but in a contemporary library it is seldom possible to hold such people forever. They are, at best, a substitute for good documentation. "If a manager can say, 'My automation librarian could leave tomorrow and I would have everything under control' then the job . . . has been well done" (White, 1990, p. 259). Without written procedures, a new manager will need to spend great energy in the discovery process, and new staff will require significantly more time to train. Even if you are the only person in systems, compile and document your procedures. Beyond the obvious value of procedures for the entire organization in the future, even a single person in a systems office will eventually need to refer back to these documents and plans.

There is no need to feel entrapped by your procedure manual; it can and should change to reflect the realities of operational changes. Updates can be done more easily in electronic formats, but there should also be a printed, dated, master copy kept in a prominent and convenient location. You will find yourself in an endless loop if the server is down and the troubleshooting documents are only on the server. You will also encounter certain documents that aren't easily incorporated into an online document but that you will want to include in your manual, such as laser printer configuration printouts. It is a good idea to include date stamps in the footer of the electronic version so that you know you're working from the most current information. Write the date and any relevant notes onto the pages of the manual. Sticky notes can easily fall out and get lost. A large three-ring binder is a convenient way to keep pages updated. Discard those that are superseded to avoid confusion.

Include both mundane and emergency information. Personnel expectations may vary in some ways from other library departments because of the nature of the work. Document this. Include inventory information. Contact information for vendors, department staff, and campus liaisons should be kept current. Your procedure manual should be a useful, living reference tool.

In addition to procedures within the department, the systems office is responsible for documenting each supported application. Documentation of any new system is of paramount importance. Include each detail of design and programming for purposes of debugging, maintenance, and the transfer of responsibility to your successor. When software is purchased, vendor supplied manuals are a good starting point. In some cases, you may need to develop one manual for technical staff and one for users of the application. Computer how-to books are a major component of the publishing industry. A wide variety of publishers market computer books for every piece of software imaginable. If the supplied software documentation isn't sufficient, shop your local or online bookstore for these third-party reference tools.

Logs and Record Keeping

Transaction and event logs can be invaluable in problem determination, statistical reporting, and troubleshooting. Transaction tracking utilities are common and relatively easy to use in contemporary network operating systems but are often neglected. Establish a regular routine for reviewing logs. If your library system software has built-in transaction log analysis, it can sometimes be used to highlight service and training deficits. It will be easier to communicate deficiencies to colleagues if your logs demonstrate supporting data. Keep paper logs to document routine procedures such as server backups. If you administer multiple servers, it can be useful to document the hardware and software history of each in a reference binder kept next to the server. In an emergency, it is often helpful to have server-specific information close at hand.

A checklist is a useful tool when updates are necessary on workstations. Without one, it is easy to overlook individual workstations in larger organizations. Checklists are most effective when they are task specific, for example, which workstations have the most recently released word processing software installed. A checklist enables multiple staff members to work on a single project efficiently. Avoid asking individual staff members to keep detailed logs of their daily activities, though. Although work logs can be a useful self-assessment tool, they can unintentionally communicate a lack of trust and tend to cause resentment.

Inventory

Some universities keep careful inventory control, depreciating computer equipment over time; others do not. In either case, the work of the systems office will benefit from a carefully kept inventory of hardware, network connections, and installed software. Beyond the obvious question of theft, it is important to know exactly where equipment is deployed because this can provide insight when troubleshooting from a remote location. Inventory data are also incredibly important when planning for the future. When planning for scheduled replacement, for example, it is useful to create a list of all hardware in a given department sorted by date of purchase.

Inventory can be tracked in a variety of ways. There are several commercial software packages that can assist. In some cases, as with Intuit Information Technology Solutions' Track-It software, inventory tracking is built into help desk software. (http://www.blueocean.com/enterprise.html) Another useful and reasonable package is Layton Technology's AuditWizard (http://www.laytontechnology.com/pages/auditwizard/audit_wizard_opt.htm). As discussed in the section on license control, AuditWizard indicates which software packages are installed but also captures data about hardware configurations. With this software, you can determine facts about a given piece of equipment and also monitor software licenses to ensure compliance with contract and licensing agreements across the enterprise.

Depending on your circumstances, it might be feasible to create an inventory using a standard relational database package such as Microsoft Access or FileMaker. If you choose this option, be sure and develop the written documentation describing in detail the conception, design, and intended procedures for its use. If you develop an inventory database, it will be less than useless if it is not kept current. Every systems tech who makes a change to equipment must be trained, encouraged, reminded, and cajoled to update the inventory if it is to be a useful tool. The benefit of some of the commercial products is their automated network discovery capability.

Statistical Reports and Analyses

Statistics are important in libraries of all sizes. From an overall management perspective, statistics fall into several areas including productivity or workflow, usage (including Web services), and benchmarking against other libraries. Although gathering statistics might seem tedious at times, collecting data to report to consortia such as the ARL can truly measure the effectiveness of a library and define its role in a cooperative environment. These data should also be used to improve the users' library experiences. Generating statistics is also part of the process of accountability for system performance. Methods of statistical generation and the use of these data is really another book in itself. This section covers just a selection of the statistical tasks of the library systems office.

A primary source of statistics is the integrated library system. Depending on the ILS software used in your library, statistics might be generated in a turnkey fashion, or reports might need to be designed and programmed. Just about any kind of statistic can be generated, from numbers of items circulated to types of searches completed in the online public access catalog.

An entirely different set of statistics can be produced from the library Web server. Many libraries are using software such as NetIQ's WebTrends to study the load on Web servers as well as to analyze how patrons are using Web services. (http://www.netiq.com/webtrends/default.asp) WebTrends software isn't terribly expensive, and because it is designed for e-commerce sites, it might produce some reports with little relevance to the library community. Most libraries "have a feeling" that lots of people are using their Web sites, but until the Web server's log files are analyzed, they cannot form an accurate idea about how patrons are using their services. WebTrends and similar products produce detailed reports including which pages are most popular, entry and exit pages, number of hits and views, and so on. These data are essential when you are developing specifications for new equipment. The size and specifications of a Web server need to be based on the typical usage you expect it to receive.

Web usage statistics can also help to improve the users' experiences when they visit the library Web site. The reports can clue the library in to the types of pages that patrons use most often as well as first and last pages they access on your system. Some reports indicate what browser and operating system clients are using to access your site. This information can provide insight when you design pages so that your site will produce the best results for the majority of your clientele. Statistical reports also provide useful information for instruction librarians who are developing handouts or classes on how to access the library's Web materials. Some database programming may be necessary to produce reports. Reports may vary in their periodicity.

Programming

It is relatively rare to encounter a library systems office that is staffed at a level that enables sustained software development activity, but it does occur in some cases. It is much more common to find systems staff designing databases or providing the occasional script, batch file, or macro for certain commercially purchased applications. Some systems departments might opt to support open source software. The developers of certain software packages freely distribute their work as "open source," meaning the code itself is available. Libraries can use this software for free if they can support it. The software might be free but likely comes with the need for local advanced support to debug problems. Open source may enable a skillful programmer to add additional sections of code or an application program interface (API) for an application instead of writing a program from the beginning. Users of open source software often collaborate on system enhancements. Examples of open source products of interest include D-Space, institutional repository software jointly developed by Hewlett-Packard and MIT, and Fedora, digital asset management software developed by the University of Virginia and Cornell University.

Managers must be sure they understand the distinction between programming and data entry. Consider hiring temporary or student staff, when possible, to perform routine data entry tasks, automating data routines whenever possible.

Changes in fashionable programming languages reflect the current needs of software development initiatives. Perl, CGI, and java are relatively recent offspring of the World Wide Web. For example, Java, introduced in 1995, temporarily delivers interactive applets that execute on a user's desktop (Gordon, 1996). Java is a secure, rich medium that has been embraced because it is platform independent. Java captured the interest of the higher education community because it has been conducive to interactive teaching and collaboration in a distributed learning environment.

Sometimes no existing software package can handle a particular task. If this is the case, approach custom programming with great trepidation. Compare the value of the resulting product with the resources needed to develop it. Longevity and maintenance issues should be considered. It is hardly worth creating a custom application if it cannot port over to new OS versions or if staffing is unavailable to maintain it. It is easy to fall into a money pit when developing custom in-house applications particularly if relevant standards are not followed.

Link Checking

One can still feel the reverberations caused by the introduction of the Mosaic Web browser in 1993. Libraries quickly adopted Web technology, partly because they did not usually have to request additional budget increments. Initially, the primary focus centered on making general library information and catalog access available in a Web environment (Branse, Elliott, & Pin, 1996). The very nature of the Web makes it easy to publish information. However, that ease also leads to information that can move or disappear quickly. Web addresses (technically referred to as uniform resource locators or URLS) can also be long and unwieldy. Even the most careful keyboardist is likely to make a typographical error with URLs. These are some of the basic reasons for checking links on Web servers.

Today, electronic resources are one of the key elements of library services. These resources are bought and sold by various vendors and server addresses are likely to change often. Because libraries were quick to embrace Web technologies and incorporate electronic resources, link-checking procedures became a critical workflow element. Many online catalogs point to Web resources based on data in the MARC 856 field but have not yet completely addressed the problem of verifying links in that field. Some content providers (notably in the government publications field) have adopted the PURL (persistent) URL method of ensuring that Web links are good. This technology uses a redirect method of checking the PURL against a database on a resolver server that maintains the correct URL. This process is invisible to most users.

The number of links incorporated into library catalogs and Web sites are growing exponentially, and links do break. Methods must be developed to track down and fix links that are not working correctly. Researchers who continually try to click on broken links will quickly become disillusioned with the libraries online resources. Link checking capabilities are often built into Web management tools such as netIQ's WebTrends (http://www.netiq.com/webtrends/default. asp) or Watchfire's WebQA (http://www.watchfire.com/products/desktop/webqa/default.aspx). Other programs, such as LinkScan (http://www.elsop. com/linkscan) are dedicated link checkers. Each of these products can automate the process of checking and repairing for broken links. Your library will want to determine procedures to specify which department is responsible for this process and when it is appropriate for software to make automatic corrections. Some human intervention will be necessary in the process.

9

Space

Physical space is a premium commodity in every library building. Everyone wants it and there is never enough to go around. When you are engaged in planning for the space needed to support information technology in a library, consider the public areas as well as the back office spaces. Walster (1993) discusses space considerations within a framework of three dimensions: location, arrangement, and function (p. 68). In her analysis, the location scale ranges from visible to invisible, the arrangement scale from formal to casual, and the function scale from pragmatic to creative. The systems office manager can use Walster's model to help structure and explain how recommendations were reached. Information from the 2003 ACRL/CNI preconference, including handouts is available at http://www.cni.org/regconfs/acrlcni2003. Creativity is many times the only way to secure the space required to support your operations. In some cases, space might be found through tools that enable virtual collaboration, but certain needs require spaces with specific physical attributes.

Facilities

A library information technology organization requires several types of spaces to support operations. The specific requirements of your organization will depend on the overall size of the library that you support as well as the range of services offered. In general, however, most operations require office space for staff members, a machine room for servers and other mission-critical equipment, room for storage, and general work space. Ideally, all of these spaces should be adjacent or within close proximity to each other. Special difficulties present themselves when your building is an older one. For example, the systems work areas need adequate electrical supplies as well as convenient elevator access. Moving print materials to remote storage is one way to increase available space for technology, but it can also be controversial. An audit of library tasks might show that certain tasks could be discontinued, outsourced, or undertaken in collaboration with consortium members. The systems office might not need to be housed in the library itself; relocation to another building might be an option to explore. It might be much more cost-effective to relocate to a newer, IT-friendly building rather than renovate space for IT in an older building.

Beyond the consideration of gross square footage, the quality of the space must be assessed. The equipment housed in a typical systems operations room is capable of generating high amounts of heat, which must be regulated to reduce the risk of fire and reduce failure rates. Consider the scalability of the heating, ventilation, and air-conditioning (HVAC) available in any space you identify. Under some circumstances, it may be necessary to add independently regulated air-conditioning, humidity, or other environmental controls to machine rooms.

Some might argue that the machine or work rooms are sufficient space for system staff members, but it is important to provide each staff member with individual office space. The office might be private or semiprivate, but dedicated office space provides staff members a quiet location to concentrate on individual tasks away from the common areas, which are full of distractions. For example, a staff member needs a place to do research on various products, to compose thoughtful responses to his or her e-mail, or to have telephone conversations with persons requesting assistance and with vendors. Providing an appropriate work space environment is one of the key elements to retaining employees and helping to maintain high levels of productivity.

In many ways, the machine or server room is the heart of the library systems organization. Here reside the servers that your clientele expect to be up and running on nearly a twenty-four hours a day/seven days a week basis. First and foremost, the machine room must be physically secure. Entry should be controlled, for example, by key, numeric code pad, or swipe card. It must also have suitable lighting, abundant electricity, and a controlled temperature and humidity environment. Depending on the amount of space available, the machine room might also serve as a common work space for your department.

The machine room or central operations facility will have a tendency to grow beyond the space you originally planned to house it. There are some steps you can take to economize on space. Rack-mounted servers can help to organize a large number of servers into a very limited amount of space. The extra space needed for cabinets and processor covers is thereby eliminated. KVM (keyboard, video, mouse) switches can channel the output display of several servers through a single monitor. There are also options for monitor-keyboard combinations that slide in and out of rack-mount spaces.

New technological solutions for almost every traditional library service are being marketed to libraries all the time. Many system vendors recommend or require the purchase of a dedicated server for optimum performance. For this reason, electricity, lighting, and environmental controls become even more important. Extra heat is a by-product of adding servers, so temperature control is essential to keep them from overheating, especially if they will be running services that are rated as mission critical in your library.

Ideally, your central operations room should have emergency generator backup power, but that is an expensive feature. If a generator isn't an option, purchase an appropriate number of uninterruptible power supply (UPS) units for your critical servers. A UPS is a battery-powered solution that will provide a short period of time after a power outage for you to close down server processes without corrupting the data on your servers. The shut down process can be automated using software should the power failure happen while the systems office is not staffed. Any UPS units you add will also generate additional heat in the operations center.

Managing a large number of computers also requires a significant amount of preparation space. When receiving a large order of new workstations, just removing the packaging generates an overwhelming amount of debris. If you plan to order new computers in large groups, be sure to have sufficient space for unpacking and storage until they are deployed.

Consider carefully how much of your old equipment to retain and what to discard. Assess the available space and its arrangement. It will be impossible to keep everything, so establish retention criteria. Many systems offices have easily established these criteria. For example, all computers with less than a Pentium III processor are to be discarded immediately upon replacement. Downstreaming computers time and time again is not a productive deployment method. Some equipment will remain useful for replacement parts if you purchased several similar units and can do repairs in-house. Periodic housekeeping and inventory schedules need to be established.

Infrastructure

There is always a weak link. In terms of technology, the weakest link is often physical infrastructure: electricity, telecommunications, and facilities. Wilson (1998) wisely warns that "stamina, persistence, and discipline" are required traits for dealing with infrastructure issues (p. 95). The first consideration is usually the physical space available and its condition. Older buildings can present issues ranging from asbestos to walls that cannot accommodate cabling, to rabbit-warren designs in which workstation security is problematic, to a leaking roof. Libraries almost never have enough space to accommodate their growing collections, making it difficult to identify space for new technology. "The amount of space at stake is so great that space planning must involve all levels of library administration and staff and seek input from library users . . . adding more computers means taking away space from some other activity . . . sensitivity to the needs of all library users is crucial" (Barclay, 2000, p. 20). When installing workstations, a generous rule of thumb is to plan on twenty-five square feet of space per workstation.

If your campus is considering a new library building, make sure to be involved in the planning process from the beginning. Discuss the library's network requirements with architects and planners. Make sure the plans are flexible to meet potential future needs. In planning for technology in new buildings, you may wish to consult the proceedings from a Stanford conference on building libraries for the twenty-first century (http://institute21.stanford.edu/programs/workshop/facilities/barrentine_tech.pdf). Jeannette Woodward's *Countdown to a New Library: Managing the Building Project* is an ALA-published resource that can also assist in designing a new building. An entire chapter is dedicated to the technological infrastructure required in a new library including telecommunication, HVAC, and electrical needs.

Be sure to include an electrical grid with sufficient electrical outlets; do not assume the trend toward mobile computing will reduce the demand for electricity. Based on observation, laptop users in academic libraries use their power adaptors even more often than they use a network connection. Never run extension cords across open floor space. Consult a certified electrician whenever adding, upgrading, or relocating computers to be sure that your building can meet the demand. Do not assume that there is sufficient electrical power just because an outlet is available. If you are fortunate enough to be involved in the design discussions for a new library building, lobby for an electrical grid across all public areas. Grid arrangements provide good flexibility when it becomes necessary to restructure internal space. You will need to consider lighting needs in your electrical planning as well.

Surge protectors and UPSs are not interchangeable devices. A UPS does not necessarily protect equipment from power surges, and a surge protector cannot keep a computer running in the event of a power failure. A power strip does not always include surge protection. Use a UPS alone or in conjunction with software that will shut the computer processes down safely in the event of a power failure. The price of a UPS unit will generally vary directly with the amount of time that its battery can support the electrical load of the equipment it runs. It may sound obvious, but removing unnecessary devices, such as monitors, from a UPS will extend the time it can run a more crucial piece of equipment.

Good network documentation includes details of every wall jack, type of cabling and connector, its closet, switch (or hub), and port. Note any associated IP address, subnet, or DHCP information, if applicable. It is helpful to label the jack clearly with indelible marker or printed labels. One labeling system to consider contains elements with the room number and plate number. Label each outlet with its own unique number. Easy-to-read labels reduce time spent in troubleshooting network malfunctions. Include documentation for wireless access points in your network inventory. The campus might be able to supply printed or online blueprints or building maps that already contain all of these data.

LAN, Phone, and Other Cabling

Although cabling can be considered part of the infrastructure of an environment, its complexity warrants a more focused discussion. Different kinds of devices usually require different kinds of cables; for example, telephones, closed circuit TV, and Ethernet all conform to their own individual standards. In the case of Ethernet cabling, advances in the ability of the channel to carry a larger number of signals probably means that the cable you have in place now might require an upgrade at some point in the future. Some of the types of cabling you might encounter include coaxial, category 3, category 5, category 6, and fiber optic. Few library systems offices are responsible for installing their own cabling. Sometimes a third-party contractor is hired; sometimes campus computing can perform this work. Because it's usually governed by legal codes, a knowledgeable specialist is a necessity. A detailed discussion of cable specifications is outside our scope here, but having a firm conceptual idea of what's going on with cabling is indispensable when managing a computing-intensive environment like today's library.

Wherever the wiring enters your building from the campus backbone, there is usually a primary wiring closet that serves as a central distribution point for all the network cables. The closet houses all of the switches, punch downs, and other equipment needed to connect the computers on your local area network (LAN) to the larger campus network and the Internet. The size of your library may necessitate other closets distributed within the building as well. When locating computers on your LAN, keep in mind that network cabling has very specific distance limitations. If you exceed them, the network connections will not perform acceptably or possibly at all. Michael and Hinnebusch (1995) provide detailed options and applications for LANs, or consult with campus networking specialists to ensure you are in line with current standards. If an external contractor installs your cabling, a good rule of thumb is to specify two data lines and one phone line for each wall plate location. Centralizing computers in a single location can be a cost savings in terms of networking but may not always meet the needs of library users.

In older buildings, asbestos can be a problem when pulling cable from the closet to the access plates. There are legal guidelines for asbestos abatement meant to ensure safe and professional removal. Take every precaution. Plan the steps you need to take to inform the public and staff that you are doing everything possible to protect their health, especially when the work happens during normal business hours. Because of the proven hazards of asbestos, it might be advisable to have your library director discuss the matter with the university attorney for advice. The campus facilities unit will usually be able to provide you with valuable guidance. Even if it means an extended wait, do not be tempted to compromise the health and safety of your staff to accomplish a job quickly.

Wireless Computing

There is a clear trend toward wireless computing on campus. It is becoming more common for laptops and PDAs (personal digital assistants) to ship with built-in networking capabilities either in the form of a network card, an infrared port, or both. Patrons are bringing their own laptops to the library and want the convenience of connecting to the network from their equipment. Wireless computing is an area where standards are only now emerging, so invest judiciously.

Wireless networks are generally designed to augment, not replace, existing wired connections. Bandwidth on a single access point is shared, so the throughput isn't as consistent as a true wired connection. Most wireless installations are based on solutions that utilize the IEEE 802.11 standard for wireless Ethernet (IEEE stands for the Institute of Electrical and Electronics Engineers). Variations of the 802.11 family refer primarily to differences in bandwidth capabilities. For example, 802.11b devices are capable to transmitting 11 megabytes per second (Mbps), whereas newer 802.11g devices permit up to 20 or more Mbps. Check out Webopedia's Wireless LAN Standards page (http://www. webopedia.com/quick_ref/WLANStandards.asp) for further details on technical standards as well as some additional resources.

The IEEE developed these protocols in an effort to establish standards for wireless networks similar to wired Ethernet networks. Wireless connectivity requires two pieces of hardware to work: an access point that is physically connected to the network and a WLAN (wireless local area network) card or device in the client machine. Indoor access points create an approximate 150-foot bubble. WLAN clients within the bubble can connect to the network via the access point. The coverage of the access point varies because of a number of variables. Walls, stone, and steel all decrease the range of an access point.

The library would be wise to consult with the campus computing office because many campuses have policies in place regulating wireless frequencies and network authentication. In fact, the library might save a great deal of time and money by partnering with the campus to offer wireless services. Costs to set up a wireless network are not necessarily astronomical, but plan carefully when deciding where wireless access is needed. For example, large, open study areas, group study rooms, or training rooms are prime candidates for public wireless installations. In staff areas, it is desirable to provide wireless access in conference rooms. In locations such as these, there are few if any physical barriers between access points and WLAN cards. This means the wireless service will be faster and more dependable as well as cost-effective. Traditional book stacks, however, are another story. The steel stacks diminish the effectiveness of wireless radio frequencies so the number of access points needed (and thus the cost) to cover a stacks area is generally higher than an open room.

A comprehensive wireless project requires an initial site survey. The site survey should analyze characteristics of the proposed coverage area including access to electricity, access point barriers, and potential access point locations. Such a survey provides the information needed to place the access points in the most practical positions. Wireless access point hardware is a common target of thieves. Make sure to hide or lock down access points to avoid losing them to theft. The site survey should also measure the signal strength from potential access points. By temporarily installing an access point, you can monitor the signal from various spots in a room. This preliminary work is essential to creating a reliable and efficient wireless network.

Security considerations need to be addressed when setting up a wireless network. Without appropriate security, any device with a WLAN card might be able to connect to your network and use it to launch malicious, hard-to-trace attacks against other computers anywhere on the Internet. There are people who seek out unsecured wireless networks and leave signs indicating the availability to others. This is sometimes called "war-chalking." To avoid the problems and liabilities this might cause, some organizations place wireless networks behind firewalls. Others require authentication the first time a WLAN card appears to the network. Some use a virtual private network (VPN) that requires each user to authenticate at each connection against a database of registered users. If the library provides wireless access to affiliated visitors, it might be necessary to secure guest logins for temporary use.

Because configuring a wireless connection is not entirely intuitive, written instructions are essential to support this kind of service. The systems office might have responsibility for configuring library-owned equipment for the wireless network, but end users should bear the responsibility for their own machines. Hands-on configuration of someone else's property may make you liable for problems, so exercise caution, especially if the laptop belongs to a patron's employer. Consider developing a form that releases the library from liability for changing system configuration of mobile computing devices.

For further information on wireless networks and associated questions, Bill Drew maintains a listserv and a Web site called the "Wireless Librarian" at http://people.morrisville.edu/~drewwe/wireless.

Ergonomics and Safety

Safety matters in the workplace. Employers have a legal and moral obligation to protect the health, safety, and welfare of workers. Safety is imperative to productivity. Hazards associated with computer work include "musculoskeletal and postural problems, upper limb disorders, eye and vision problems, stress, reproductive hazards, and some others" (Morris & Dyer, 1998, pp. 32–33).

Ergonomics (the physical interaction and design of workplace and operator) and anthropometrics (the study of the structural differences in humans) increase in importance when people spend prolonged amounts of time sitting at computer stations. Repetitive motion injuries and vision problems are associated with increased computer usage. Take the necessary steps to minimize the health risks for both public and staff. Barclay (2000) suggests two basic rules for good ergonomics: users need to be able to shift their position frequently, and adjustable furniture is more comfortable.

Loose cables are a common hazard associated with system installations. Some furniture suppliers offer built-in cable runs, which are useful for keeping cabling neat and off the floor. Cable ties are also a worthwhile investment but can sometimes slow down troubleshooting. Never run cables across walking areas. Find a solution that will keep people from tripping over cables and wiring.

Morris and Dyer (1998) do a thorough job of explaining the health risks associated with computers and offering some solutions. Many campuses have an ergonomics office that can assist in addressing ergonomics related concerns. Additional information about ergonomics and technology is available online from at the Occupational Safety and Health Administration's Computer Workstation eTool site (http://www.osha.gov/SLTC/etools/computerworkstations/index.html) or Typing Injury FAQ (http://www.tifaq.com).

Computers require furniture. Furniture should be safe, durable, and aesthetically pleasing. It should allow open sight lines from services areas, both for the purpose of security and for ease in gaining assistance from library staff. This also allows adequate ventilation of the equipment. Most library staff members will be able to work using standard office furniture. If the systems department is responsible for public computing furniture, there are several issues to consider. Areas that receive heavy use might require kiosk-type furniture allowing users to stand at a workstation for a short period of time. Patrons who use library workstations for long periods of time might be more comfortable in carrels designed for computers. A library's user population, available space, and facility infrastructure will likely define the type of furniture that is needed. Furniture manufacturers and suppliers are regular exhibitors at library conferences. Most would be happy to add your library to their mailing lists. Browse their Web sites to get an idea of their offerings. Other considerations affecting the purchase of furniture include ADA (Americans with Disabilities Act) compliance, sound ergonomics, maintenance accessibility, and cable management. A useful resource on ADA compliance by Wright and Davie (1991) is called *Serving the Disabled: A How-To-Do-It Manual for Librarians*.

Research and New Technologies

Academic libraries must make every attempt to anticipate the expectations and demands of the campus community and stay ahead of them in their adoption of new technologies. "The potential benefits of each new technology come from asking how libraries can use [it] to accomplish what they are not already doing" (Sweeney, 1994, p. 80). The quest to expand services that complement their missions of education and research has a tendency to increase the library's receptivity to new tool sets. According to Gorman (2003), "It is a feature of society as a whole, and libraries in particular, that the newest technology is always received with irrational ardor and is always seen as transformational" (p. xi). We should consider exploring, evaluating, and introducing new tools as essential responsibilities for the systems office.

It is imperative that library systems managers support and encourage these activities. Make it easy for employees to experiment with new products and technologies even if in a controlled environment. Designating funds for the purchase of new software and hardware and encouraging systems staff to evaluate it is sometimes perceived as "playing." Nevertheless, this is an important part of the way we learn and advance new technologies. "Local 'R&D' by librarians-turned-computer-jocks is not wasted investment on automation amateurism" (Nielsen, 1989, p. 110). Technology staff members generally enjoy the prospect of learning about new software, sometimes to the point of neglecting other responsibilities. It may become necessary for systems managers to clarify boundaries with more formal guidelines that stipulate criteria for evaluation and reporting on conclusions. Nielsen (1989) suggests that "Top library management should be prepared to articulate a research and development agenda" (p. 109). A checklist for evaluating new technologies can be found in a later section of this chapter.

Encourage and support individual exploration and experimentation by providing software tools while taking appropriate steps to safeguard data. Creative use of technological tools can arise in unexpected quarters and can then be shared across a department or within the entire library. They may even occasionally achieve some measure of commercial success. This is a bottom-up-driven development and empowerment model. Many automated library systems were developed in-house (e.g., CARL at the University of Denver, the Library Computer System at the University of Illinois, NOTIS at Northwestern University, and MELVYL at the University of California, Berkeley). Although the scope of the contemporary ILS makes it impractical to develop, commercialize, or support these systems in most cases, in-house systems still proliferate when a specific need is not adequately met by the marketplace. Today, other systems fall into this category. For example, the ILLiad interlibrary loan management system was initially developed by Virginia Tech. CONTENTdm, a popular digital asset management tool, was created by an engineering professor at the University of Washington.

Speculation about what the library of the future might look like is often an emotionally charged debate, especially when library budgets hang in the balance. Some university administrators have justified reducing library budgets because they believe that everything the library can provide is available without cost on the Internet. This is only one example of a serious misunderstanding about the direction that technological progress is taking. Both librarians and systems managers must learn how to respond with persuasive and well-supported arguments to this naïve point of view. Researching and evaluating new technology is a proactive way to anticipate and plan for the library of the future. "Some see the library of the future as nothing more than a kind of switching station in a network environment" (Lancaster & Sandore, 1997, pp. 239–40), but there will always be an important role for libraries and librarians in terms of organization, identification, and access to information. This becomes even truer in light of the exponential growth in the volume of information enabled by the Internet. The School of Information Management and Systems at the University of California at Berkeley has undertaken a fascinating study of how much information exists in different formats. The 2003 study (available at http://www.sims.berkeley.edu/research/projects/how-much-info-2003) proposes that size of the Internet is more than 532,000 terabytes.

Training for public service staff in newly deployed technologies should not be neglected. In most cases, they are the people who field the brunt of questions from the public. Kalin (1991) observes that immediately after implementation of a new service, most libraries encounter a deluge of questions that eventually taper down (p. 202). Systems staff could offer to "shadow" at public desks during the early phases of a new service to assist in the transition. "In the end, whatever is the domain of the specialist will become the domain of line staff. An uninvolved and uninformed staff will not be ready to take on this role" (Barber, 1996, pp. 711–12).

Teaching and Learning in a Web-based World

Life before the Internet, and specifically the World Wide Web, is nothing more than a dim memory for most of us. For higher education, the Web and its associated technologies opened a floodgate of new methods for information sharing and collaboration. Increasing collaboration between librarians and teaching faculty is a logical step because librarians are experts at collecting, selecting, and organizing information and faculty are experts at distilling and explicating it to learners. Collaboration benefits the entire academy by creating a diverse environment for learners as well as promoting information sharing and guiding the learning process (Connell & Franklin, 1994).

We are witnessing an increasing number of teaching and learning centers on college campuses whose stated missions vary widely, but that strive to integrate technology, content, and teaching in ways that maximize learner effectiveness. "As more faculty members and students are encouraged to use technology for teaching and learning, they expect to accomplish more, and they quickly discover they need more help. The capacity of academic support services to provide help usually falls farther behind as expectations rise. Costs go up and the 'Support Service Crisis' gets worse" (Gilbert, 2001).

To move forward from collections of information to genuine knowledge, learners must internalize stimuli and integrate concepts to the point that they can describe and defend reasoned conclusions on their own. In Sweeney's (1994) view, "learning must result from learner-initiated reading, watching videos, listening to tapes, interacting with multimedia, and asking questions or experimenting" (p. 73). No matter how much technical support becomes available on campus, the exponential increase in the size of the Web has greatly decreased an individual's ability to retrieve credible or exhaustive content with any degree of precision. This is easily demonstrated by the preference of many students to begin their research with Google and use the first few results in a retrieval set that may number in the tens of thousands. One of the roles of the university, the faculty, and the library is to provide learners with more precise and reliable strategies and tools to distill the knowledge available from Web-based resources.

Mission-Critical Technologies

As new technologies are adopted, some become critical links for access to the content of collections. Web servers and workstations may fall into this category—servers because most access (even to traditional paper resources) is now mediated by Web OPACs and workstations because they provide access to information from the Web servers. Ironically, without the server and the workstation, it would be extraordinarily difficult to locate much of anything in a library's permanent paper collections. Few libraries maintain any of their older finding technologies such as card catalogs or paper printouts. Once committed to the server and workstation as the means of access to our libraries, we need to understand that their failure could be disastrous.

Collections that are "born digital" also imply critical technologies, but with a whole set of their own issues for data migration and refreshment. Digital collections rely on the technologies under which they were created. To keep them viable, vigilance is required to ensure that they are readable within the framework of an advancing technological infrastructure. Systems managers and administrators must maintain an awareness of the resources being created and stored on servers for which they are responsible. Smart management (including security and disaster recovery plans) are crucial to the preservation and integrity of digital collections.

Evaluation of New Technologies

The introduction to this chapter stressed the essential role the systems office plays in the implementation of new technologies. This role is inescapable in light of the dizzying pace in the release of new operating systems alone. Increasingly, operating systems, especially the Windows series of operating systems, are an umbrella for new application development and workstation features. When new workstations arrive in the library, they may be configured in radically different ways from those that the library previously purchased. To support these inevitable changes, as well as new technologies that are released independently, systems staff must develop a continual habit of detailed exploration and analysis. Just because other libraries are adopting a new technology doesn't mean it will function correctly in your environment. We offer an adapted version of Barclay's (2000) checklist in Figure 10.1 as a guide in the evaluation of new technologies.

Impacts and Applications of International Standards

Standards represent sets of rules that facilitate wider interoperability of new technologies than would otherwise be possible. When more than one group views a new technology as lucrative and more people become involved in developing applications, a single standard is slower to emerge. This can create artificial barriers to product enhancement because developers must address each product separately instead of as a class of products. Standards help to mature technologies. When a library purchases a product that is proprietary, that is, not based on a universal or industry standard, it has the potential of limiting the growth and utility of the original purchase. Worse, if the company that originally provided the product goes out of business, it might be necessary to start over

☐ Is installation straightforward?

☐ Does it crash or freeze?

☐ Does it conflict with existing software?

☐ Does it run well on our workstations?

☐ Does it run well on our network?

☐ Do all the features work?

☐ Have we tested all features?

☐ Will it work for multiple simultaneous users?

☐ Will it work for remote users?

☐ Does printing work?

☐ Are there security holes?

☐ How good is vendor technical support?

☐ How good is online and context-sensitive help?

☐ Is the interface self-explanatory and easy to use?

☐ How good is the documentation?

☐ Does it do what we bought it to do?

Figure 10.1. Checklist for testing new software (Barclay, 2000, p. 4).

from the beginning with a different product. Connell and Franklin (1994) caution, however, to balance standards against the ability of users to understand them (p. 619). For a discussion of incorporation of standards into the purchase of an automated library system, consult http://www.niso.org/standards/resources/RFP_Writers_Guide.pdf. Helping colleagues understand and implement standards is one of the functions of the systems librarian.

Several key organizations engage in the development of standards important to libraries. Among these are the National Information Standards Organization (NISO) and the American National Standards Institute (ANSI). Because innovations often appear in the marketplace before there are standards to guide them, the standards usually develop in response to new technologies. The effectiveness of a technology is occasionally limited subsequent to the adoption of the set of standards that pertain to it. Examples of standards we find in libraries include Z39.50, OpenURL, 802.11, Machine Readable Cataloging (MARC), and Extensible Markup Language (XML). New standards are constantly in development. For example, the Dublin Core Metadata Element Set is an ISO/NISO standard that addresses description of Internet and other resources. Similarly, Encoded Archival Description (EAD) is a standard method of encoding archival finding aids for Internet search and retrieval.

Z39.50 is a standard protocol that facilitates what is sometimes referred to as broadcast searching across disparate database applications, while returning the result set to a user in a uniformly familiar display. The original vision of what would be possible under Z39.50 has not been fully realized, because the retrieval results have had to sacrifice some of the richness of the source data in return for uniformity of the display. This ANSI/NISO standard allows network data access from Z39.50 compliant servers to be accessed across dissimilar user displays. Machovec (1991) provides a description of the development of the Z39.50 development process but cautions that automation vendors may choose to comply with the standard at differing levels.

The emerging OpenURL standard is potentially important because it will allow systems and their users to link from an online search to several different services capable of providing the resource itself. An example of a commercial product that uses OpenURL is SFX. A resolver server is employed that is able to identify the resource in full-text online format, to identify it in a local library catalog, to initiate an interlibrary loan request for it, or to purchase it from a vendor. The standard will define the general framework to bundle specific packages of contextual metadata and transport them over a network. It will provide details about the core properties that can be used.

Typically, the standard developing bodies, which include NISO, ISO, and the IEEE, submit their work for public comment before finalization with detailed instructions about how to comment. This process can take a long time to complete. For example, part of the new OpenURL standard was out for comment in the first months of 2003. After the comment period, the standard was released for a trial period in early 2004 and then posted for ballot and review. Later in 2004, the standard was approved and being readied for publication. The latest versions of OpenURL documents are posted at http://library.caltech.edu/openurl/Public_Comments.htm.

Another example of a standard is 802.11 for wireless networks. The development of the 802.11 standard was an interesting process because it contraindicated some elements of a popular piece of production software called Bluetooth. Parts of the 802.11 standard continue to be developed.

So much detail is available concerning the MARC standard that it is not necessary to discuss it in detail here. We can and should mention that MARC is important in libraries because it was one of the earliest technology standards, enabling the transition from card to automated catalogs. In brief terms, the MARC standard divides each descriptive bibliographic record into its field, subfield, and indicator elements. However, ML has the potential to exceed the impact of MARC on librarianship (Tennant, 2002, p. vii) because the XML standard can describe each element of entire documents. This technology has far-reaching implications for enriching traditional library services ranging from interlibrary loan to the online catalog, as well as expanding emerging services such as digital collections and online publishing.

Portals

Portals are dynamic Web sites that allow users to customize and personalize content and services. The massive amount of information available via the Internet means that users need a tool such as a portal to deliver focused information resources. The ability to personalize one's learning environment enhances the educational experience. This has been recognized for years before the technology was available to implement such services. "The computer's greatest promise as an educational aid depends on its use as a personalized environment for learning" (Turkle, 1991, p. 8). Turkle's prophetic pronouncement was published before the Internet and the Web permeated academia and reflects a time when universities and libraries were just beginning to integrate technology into their curricula and services. Nevertheless, perhaps no statement could have better predicted the advent of portals.

Portals have a variety of definitions and incarnations but all provide some mechanism for users to customize or personalize information resources. Jafari (2003) distinguishes between a Web page and a portal using the analogy of a newspaper. Anyone buying a newspaper gets the same stories and pictures, but a portal is different because it recognizes a visitor's role and preferences (p. 9). Many commercial Web sites utilize portals to personalize visits. Regular visitors to the online retailer amazon.com can log onto the Web site and receive recommendations based on previous purchases. News channels such as MSNBC.com (http://msnbc.com) offer the opportunity to customize visits by tailoring content based on a user's ZIP code or other preferences. Portal initiatives are strong among academic Web sites as well. Campuses are developing portals to provide one-stop experiences for students. Many are choosing software called Campus Pipeline because of the way it can be integrated into administrative campus database systems. uPortal is a popular open source alternative. By logging into a single Web site, students are able to navigate to personalized academic, social, financial, or other information. If the library participates as a partner in the process of campus portal development, library representatives would be wise to advocate automating as much password pass through access as possible for library services like book renewals and reserve reading lists. Portals also offer a way to broadcast targeted information to specific group. A university might, for example, push a message about graduation deadlines to all students identified as seniors in their registration database.

Library portals offer similar types of personalization. Individuals can potentially verify which library materials they have checked out, determine the amounts of their outstanding fines, renew materials, save their preferred catalog searches, and receive electronic notification when material relevant to their research interests arrive in the library. Perhaps the most popular function of a library portal is the ability to search across a variety of user-selected databases. This ability vastly improves the searching experience for users as full-text journals become increasingly available from a vast and growing number of content providers and consolidators. Users are coming to expect the ability to customize and personalize their Web visits. A Library and Information Technology Association (LITA) panel in 1999 identified this as the leading technology trend for libraries (Lakos & Gray, 2000).

Portal development requires a commitment from the library. Portal products require significant expertise to configure and are often costly to purchase. The impact of starting up a portal on the library systems office is similar to that of implementing an integrated library system. A separate server is generally needed to run the portal software. The portal software itself will require a great deal of configuration and possibly some programming expertise. Because portal software interacts with a large number of remote resources, the systems office should plan an extended period of testing prior to deployment so that the impact on network performance will be clearly understood.

A variety of vendors provide library software that reflects the influence of portals. Some of these products are sold by traditional library system vendors. Examples include ExLibris' SFX product (http://www.sfxit.com) and Innovative Interfaces' Millennium Access Plus or MAP suite (http://www.iii.com). Generally these products will work in an environment whether or not the library also uses the vendor's integrated library system products.

Digital Library Initiatives

Some of the trendiest new developments in libraries are centered on their digital library initiatives. Digital initiatives encompass a wide range of projects from digitizing print, sound, or video collections for online access, to creating institutional digital repositories of knowledge based on content that is owned and created by the college or university. Digital initiatives require librarywide planning and collaboration as well as additional technical skills. All aspects of digital initiatives cannot be covered here. We address the highlights of digital library support here and provide additional sources of information.

The impetus for digital initiative projects in the library may come from a department or branch or from within the systems office. In many libraries, the systems office takes a leadership role by coordinating and managing the digital library. Some systems departments even have digital initiatives units. Even if this is not the case, the systems office can certainly expect to provide various levels of support for these projects. In their early stages, the systems office can expect to provide or support a facility with appropriate equipment to digitize designated collections. While off-the-shelf flatbed scanners might be able to support some projects, others will require more expensive, specialized equipment with the ability to digitize larger or three-dimensional objects. Large-format scanners, book scanners, and digital cameras are just some of the tools required to reformat certain types of materials. Every staff member involved in these projects might want dedicated equipment on their desk, but the systems office might determine that a more cost-effective use of such resources would be to centralize them within a scan center or digital initiatives laboratory. A central lab leverages the cost of potentially expensive equipment among several projects and is also easier for the systems office to support.

Digital initiatives require a specific set of skills. Depending on staffing levels, this expertise might already be available in the library. The formula for providing support to digital initiatives will vary based on the nature of the project as well as available funding. Some libraries have chosen to outsource much of the actual digital reformatting. There are some private companies as well as some nonprofit organizations that are willing to contract for the production work. Student labor is another possible option. When using student workers, however, you will need to clearly define the methods and standards for digitization to ensure that items are converted in a consistent manner. Very large libraries may have a digital library unit; the unit may report to the systems office. This scenario allows both librarians and support staff the opportunity to study and apply best practices in digitization. In some instances, libraries are hiring systems librarians who specialize in digital projects. Like digital projects themselves, no single solution is perfect, and the ideal situation for your library will depend on funding and the nature of the projects underway.

The systems office will likely be asked to provide advice on how to digitize particular objects. This might range from agreeing on specific pixel sizes for digital images to suggesting the size of audio or video files destined for streaming via the Web. Each project is different, and the approach will depend on a number of factors, including the condition of the original collection, funding, and whether the collection is being digitized for access, preservation, or both. In areas for which the standards are not yet clear, best practices are being described by leaders in the area. The tools and organizations listed at the end of this section can be useful starting places for making decisions such as these.

After digitization, metadata creation is the other vital element of digital initiatives. This process is another example of how digitization projects require collaboration throughout the library. Examples of metadata standards include encoded archival description (EAD), Dublin Core, and MARC. The systems office might provide advice on methods and software products for including metadata, but the cataloging department will probably wish to provide input to ensure that the metadata has the potential for interoperability and integration among all digital projects where different metadata schemes have been used. If the digitization is done in-house, metadata can be assigned to each object at the same time. If it is outsourced, developing the metadata will require a separate step. At this point, we will risk an opposing viewpoint concerning the growing acceptance of metadata, even though its utility is generally unquestioned when faced with overwhelming quantities of digitized materials. Uncritical use of metadata may be controversial among certain conservative catalogers who see it as an abridgement of traditional cataloging formats. Gorman (2003) expresses skepticism that metadata could ever provide the controlled vocabulary and access points generally expected in traditional cataloging.

The storage requirements associated with digital initiatives can be massive. Because digital initiatives are often project-based, ask the project manager for a size requirement estimate and a future growth estimate so that the systems office can make appropriate plans to accommodate storage needs. Although each project is predictable to some extent, the overall program may not be. A flexible storage growth plan is necessary. The systems office will need to provide an array of reliable storage and backup mechanisms. There are many ways to handle this, and, like other elements of these projects, the best solution needs to reflect your own environment. When digitization projects are undertaken in a consortial environment, storage issues may only bear an indirect impact on the systems office, but increased collaboration will be necessary. In the last few years, the cost of disk drives has decreased, and their capacity has increased. This is positive news for libraries engaging in digital initiatives. Several gigabytes of storage can be purchased in a standard server for less than $5,000. Network-attached storage devices such as Snap servers also provide large amounts of space at a relatively low cost. The largest projects might require a more expensive but dependable storage method such as a storage area network (SAN). A SAN is an enterprise-wide storage solution that combines the resources of several servers across the network.

Because digital initiatives have the potential to create massive amounts of date, storage solutions require extra consideration. Backup procedures must be integrated into your storage solution. Major hardware failures, while unlikely, do occur. Hackers will find the storage space if it is not adequately protected. These issues might be addressed in an enterprise solution such as a SAN but if data are stored on servers or network attached devices, backup might need to be handled differently. The systems office should be able to integrate this into the backup routines of other servers discussed in the Server Management section. Keep in mind that when disk storage is larger, the backup system will need to be fast enough to handle them at an established rate of frequency. Some digitization programs store archival data on CD-ROM, but the life span of CDs dictates that eventually the data will need to be migrated to another medium. Some other options in use include high-quality "gold" CDs, DVDs, and tape. Because digital storage technologies are constantly changing and developing, be sure to investigate current best practices before deciding on a specific media.

While still in the early stages of a project, it is important to think about how to preserve the data that are created and to ensure some measure of future integrity. The standards that apply today for digitizing information may not be applicable in five, ten, or fifteen years. Unfortunately, this is one of the big unknowns in the field. Because it is impractical to redigitize collections, the best advice is to observe current standards to the extent possible and avoid proprietary formats. If, for example, a project creates .tiff images as archival images, the systems office needs to be prepared for the possibility that, in the future, they may need to migrate these images to another format.

Knowledge and experience about digital initiatives has grown over the last several years. There are many places to gather information to help technology managers make informed decisions about the various aspects of particular projects. One such national organization is the nonprofit Council on Library and Information Resources (CLIR). A private organization with relatively expensive membership fees, CLIR's mission is to ensure that all types of information resources are available to future students, scholars, researchers, and the public. Visit CLIR (http://www.clir.org) to read their excellent set of white papers. The Digital Library Federation (DLF) is a consortium of institutions at the leading edge of digital initiatives. The DLF Web site (http://www.diglib.org) provides some useful resources. Be aware that many DLF services are limited to members. Finally, NINCH's (National Initiative for a Networked Cultural Heritage) *Guide to Good Practice* (http://www.nyu.edu/its/humanities/ninchguide) is another important resource with detailed step-by-step information.

Other organizations have been formed around the country to provide local support for digital initiatives. Two examples of this are the Colorado Digitization Program (http://www.cdpheritage.org) and the Florida Center for Library Automation Digital Library Services unit (http://www.fcla. edu/dlini/dlinipg.html). These groups work to provide information on digital initiatives to libraries and other organizations in their states and regions. Both have extensive resources posted on their Web sites and offer training and support to member libraries.

There are also several well-known and recommended training opportunities. Two of the oldest are the School for Scanning and Cornell's Moving Theory into Practice: Digital Imaging for Libraries and Archives workshop. The School for Scanning is sponsored by the Northeast Document Conservation Center (NEDCC), a large, nonprofit organization that provides preservation advice and services to libraries, museums, archives, and other organizations. Founded in 1973, the NEDCC's first mission was to assist with preservation of paper and other materials. As digitization became more pervasive, NEDCC became a leader in that arena as well. The School for Scanning is offered once or twice a year in various locations. The faculty of the school is composed of a wide range of leaders and experts in digital initiatives. NEDCC points out that this is not a technician-training setting, although technical topics are discussed. The conference is an excellent opportunity for managers or administrators who are new to digital initiatives. NEDCC provides free online access to an outgrowth of the School for Scanning, the *Online Handbook for Digital Projects* at http://www. nedcc.org/digital/dighome.htm.

Another leader in digital initiatives is the Cornell University Library. For several years, Cornell offered the Moving Theory into Practice: Digital Imaging for Libraries and Archives workshop. This workshop was a hands-on technical training experience for those involved in the creation and preservation of digital information. Even though this workshop is no longer offered, the major text that grew out of these workshops, Anne R. Kenney and Oya Y. Rieger's book, *Moving Theory into Practice*, remains one of the authoritative guides for libraries preparing to embark on digital projects (Research Libraries Group, 2000). Today, Cornell offers a new workshop, Digital Preservation Management: Implementing Short-Term Strategies for Long-Term Problems (http://www.library.cornell.edu/iris/dpworkshop), which has the goal of fostering practical and responsible stewardship of digital assets.

Mobile Computing

As technology has matured, many have observed a trend toward miniaturization, as well as reductions in cost. Mobile computing devices such as laptops, tablet computers, and PDAs are now affordable for mainstream computer users. The functionality and power of desktop computers that ten years ago cost thousands of dollars now cost just hundreds and fit in your shirt pocket. In a wireless-enabled environment, many of these devices are shipped Internet-ready. RFID (radio frequency identification) technology combines a radio signal with a microchip into a tag that can be placed in a book and is capable of tracking providing inventory information for that piece. The library systems office should plan to support these devices because of their increasing popularity and availability.

The first decision is what to buy. If a user is planning to employ a portable device as a replacement for a desktop computer, a laptop is currently one of the most sensible options. Today's laptop and notebook computers are small, powerful, and relatively inexpensive. Laptops are practical for users who work, teach, or make presentations in multiple locations. Tablet computers are emerging as a powerful teaching tool because of their ability to incorporate ink technology, which enables handwritten annotations over text. It can be used instead of a keyboard to translate handwriting into type within documents. Sketches and drawings can also be incorporated. In the primary work location, a docking station complete with monitor and keyboard can be deployed, essentially converting the laptop into a full desktop device. Many users are content with a laptop and won't need to dock. Users who require minimal computing power when away from a primary work location might opt for a PDA. A PDA provides some computing capabilities as well as the ability to synchronize with another machine, such as the user's primary desktop computer.

The marketplace is full of vendors of mobile computing equipment. Selecting a vendor and model will depend on requirements specific to individuals within the organization. Most computer manufacturers sell laptop models. If your organization has a relationship with a preferred vendor, that might be the best option. Some organizations purchase one brand of desktop computer and another brand of laptop computers. This is dependent on experience as well as local purchasing requirements and costs. Laptops generally ship with either the Windows or Macintosh operating system, so they should fit into most library environments. When evaluating PDAs for purchase, however, the operating system becomes a more important element of the purchasing decision. PDAs are available with standard operating systems such as Palm or Microsoft PocketPC, but there are other mobile devices with proprietary operating systems that might not fit well into the library computing environment. Consider how PDAs will synchronize with local PCs and the software running on those PCs when making a decision. For example, a PDA running a proprietary operating system might not synchronize well with Microsoft Outlook desktop clients. These issues are constantly changing as mobile hardware and software matures.

Personal organization is probably the most basic function of handheld computing devices. Even novice users can use, for example, a PDA to keep a personal calendar and organize tasks. Consult with users to determine the best hardware and software fit for their individual needs. Palm requires third-party software to synchronize e-mail attachments, whereas PocketPC may be less stable and require more frequent rebooting under some circumstances. The systems office might even test some mobile devices and inform users which devices work best in the local environment. This is particularly important if the library doesn't purchase these devices but only supports user-owned devices. Users might find bargain-basement deals on PDAs that they think will synchronize just fine with their computer or with the campus calendaring system. If they don't, the user will be unhappy, and the systems office is faced with a predictable and avoidable problem. The systems office needs to be proactive in support for PDAs to avoid a splintered and ineffectual support scenario.

Mobile devices are gaining popularity in many college classrooms. Several vendors offer a cart complete with a wireless access point and several laptop computers. This may be a viable option for libraries that want to provide a hands-on learning experience for students but don't have the space or funds to maintain a permanent computing lab. Such carts are available for both PC and Macintosh platforms. The instructor connects the cart to the network, and the wireless access point provides network access to the mobile devices. Clearly the systems office will need to provide support to ensure the devices work as expected and run the software required.

Some libraries also loan laptops to users. This is a popular service, particularly for users who want the convenience of a laptop but cannot afford one. A library might decide to offer this service or perhaps partner with the campus computing organization to do so. In either case, the systems office must be aware of the support requirement so that the equipment is always ready for users. One approach is to load a fresh desktop image each time the device is returned. Extra batteries help to ensure that mobile devices will always be fully charged. Security and liability concerns must also be considered.

Users will also bring personally owned laptops to the library. The systems office may need to work with the library administration or public services units to determine what level of support or facilities will be provided for mobile computing users. Laptop users will generally find a power outlet wherever one is available. Some users go as far as disconnecting network cables from public workstations and connecting their laptops to the in-house network. These are support issues that the systems office likely needs to address within the library as a whole. For example, is it feasible in your environment to establish a laptop computing area complete with power and network outlets? Can all of the study carrels and tables in the library provide power and network capability for mobile devices?

Some libraries have been experimenting with the use of PDAs for in-house tasks. For example, PDAs might enhance inventory or circulation activities. The scope of these functions will largely depend on the library infrastructure. An inventory list might be loaded to a PDA to enable an employee to search for items in the stacks. Notes about the items could be added and the data analyzed later. Depending on the model of the PDA, it might be possible to attach a barcode reader to it. A variety of inventory projects for books or even bar-coded equipment could be handled in this manner. Using PDAs for live connections to the library ILS might be a bit trickier because traditional stacks locations are among the most difficult to provide with consistent and reliable wireless access. Library staff may create the most demand as well as the most innovative applications for PDAs, so the systems office should be prepared to work with these users and provide support. Emerging applications of PDAs in libraries are highlighted in a special section of the final 2003 issue of *Library Hi Tech*.

Mobile computing has made what appear to be permanent inroads in libraries. Mobile devices will become smaller and more affordable, so the opportunities for library applications will broaden. More vendors will also enter the marketplace. Some mainstream computer manufacturers such as Dell are now building and selling their own line of PDAs. New styles of devices will also become available. Tablet PCs are among the newest. These devices offer flexibility combined with computing power that can rival a desktop unit. Their operating systems facilitate new ways to transform handwriting and voice input into text, layers of handwritten notes over text, as well as many other innovations. These units constantly seem to get lighter, and their battery life is increasing.

Web Logs

Web logs, known as "blogs" for short, are a kind of an online Web diary, providing information on topics that interest the author of the site. Some sites support the RSS (RDF Site Summary or Rich Site Summary) protocol, which is an XML-based method of preparing news or other content for automatic distribution to subscribers via the Web.

Blogs vary in content. Some are general and others very specific in focus. They can also range from formal to extremely informal in nature. Some libraries are using blogs to replace traditional newsletters or columns. They have also been used as marketing or public relations tools.

Examples of blogs that might be of specific interest to systems librarians include the following:

http://www.lisnews.com/

http://dmoz.org/Reference/Libraries/Library_and_Information_Science/ Weblogs/

http://www.teleread.org/blog/

http://eprintblog.crimsonblog.com/

http://www.handheldlib.blogspot.com/

http://usrlib.info

http://www.theshiftedlibrarian.com/

Videoconferencing

It is commonly said that the world has changed since the terror attacks of September 11. Airline travel has become more challenging. The effects of the economy and federal budget requirements have reduced state budgets. State budget cuts have often meant reductions to higher education allocations. For these and other reasons, videoconferencing is a technology that may soon see increased use in libraries, especially for tasks such as candidate interviews and participation in workshops and other group meetings. Videoconferencing can enable people in Internet-accessible locations to participate in meetings, collaborate, and share information over the Internet or within an intranet. Only one computer needs to have the program to be shared, and all participants can work on the document simultaneously. Videoconferencing allows participants to place calls using directory servers, conferencing servers, and Web pages.

Microsoft NetMeeting, which ships with some versions of the Windows operating system, is an example of widely available videoconferencing software. It provides both audio and video channels, so that even if you don't have a camera that can transmit video, you can still receive video calls. Entry-level Web cameras begin around $20, putting them within easy reach of most budgets. NetMeeting also supports live, encrypted Chat. Chat is discussed further in the following section. Using the Whiteboard, you can explain concepts by diagramming information, using a sketch, or displaying graphics. You can also copy areas of your desktop or windows and paste them to the Whiteboard. WebEx online meetings and Timbuktu are other examples of software that may have some potential as interactive educational tools.

Interactive Chat

Chat is software that enables synchronous, text-based communication among one or more users. Participation in an online chat happens simultaneously and in real time, without the delays associated with the asynchronous environment of e-mail or other methods of sharing written communication. Distance education increasingly utilizes both synchronous and asynchronous learning environments. BlackBoard and WebCT, widely used course management systems, incorporate both e-mail and chat, among many other features. Both individual libraries and consortia are exploring chat as a tool to provide virtual reference service. Some are concerned that the decreasing numbers of reference desk transactions require them to reposition reference service. Interactive chat popularity is growing quickly as a means of providing online reference service. Among ARL libraries, Ronan and Turner (2002) found that sixty-seven had undertaken chat reference service as of December 2002.

Along with simultaneous communication, other features that interactive chat software may support include push-page technology, co-browsing, statistics gathering, and the potential for automatic tracking of frequently used resources. These features are important to the reference process for obvious reasons. Other factors that may influence the selection of chat software include the ability to restrict access to targeted populations, easy access for users, and the ability to use a conventional Web browser without downloading or installing additional software.

The systems office might be called on to evaluate software, obtain quotes, understand and configure the software, and support and train participants. Systems personnel might need to host a chat server to support live reference service. Chat software can range from freeware to expensive, full-service products hosted on remote vendor servers.

Some examples of chat software or service providers include the following:

Microsoft's MSN Messenger (http://messenger.msn.com)

Internet Relay Chat (IRC) (http://www.mirc.com)

LSSI Virtual Reference Toolkit (http://www.vrtoolkit.net)

OCLC QuestionPoint (http://www.questionpoint.org)

Docutek VRL Plus (http://www.docutek.com/products/vrl/index.html)

Wiki is a recent technology that shares some of the more superficial characteristics of chat but is somewhat less synchronous. *Wiki* is the Hawaiian word for "quick." Technologies such as wiki permit anyone to edit a live Web page or add a page to a site. If more than one person is working on a page at a time, the first person who saves the file preserves their changes. The drawback of such an arrangement, of course, is that anything on a page could also be deleted or changed by someone with malicious intent, but there may be potential for remote teaching and learning with this technology.

Intranets

Most libraries have spent considerable staff time and effort developing a strong Web presence for the public. Many, however, have not spent a similar amount of time on creating a Web presence for staff purposes. In the early years of library Web sites, many organizations chose to integrate resources most useful for their own staff into the public Web presence. Today, a library might be wise to investigate the possibilities of an intranet. An intranet is essentially a private network for the creating organization. It doesn't require a separate physical network but is generally restricted to a particular set of users. This can be accomplished by password or IP address authentication or firewall protection.

Intranets have been popular among businesses for several years. Companies use private Web servers to share confidential or proprietary data such as training materials, trade secrets, or research and development tools. Libraries can follow the same model to provide restricted access to resources that might not be applicable or even licensed for the general public. Although a library might limit the number of people authorized to publish to the public Web server, all interested staff members might be allowed to publish to the intranet Web server.

Many staff-related resources are well suited for intranet publication. For example, a library staff handbook is not necessarily confidential information, but its usefulness for the public is limited. Such a resource can be easily stored and maintained on an intranet. Library staff involved in professional activities might require Web space or services for their work. Committee Web pages or surveys developed by staff members might not be appropriate for the library Web site, but an intranet could provide the space needed for this work. Libraries might purchase licensed professional working tools such as the Library of Congress' Cataloger's Desktop. An intranet can be a convenient way to provide access to this service in-house while restricting broader access. The intranet can also be used as a development or prototype server for Web content that staff is creating for the public Web site.

Document Delivery

In this discussion, document delivery designates the full text of articles delivered electronically; conventional returnables are outside our scope. Document delivery is an essential service component for all libraries; interlibrary loans and other forms of document delivery supplement local collections. Document delivery systems are able to supply a digital copy of a published article in response to a user request. A user in this sense can be either a library or an individual. The material can then be forwarded via fax, mail, or in digital format.

Electronic document delivery can be much quicker than the more traditional interlibrary loan process. Interlibrary loan departments are integrating these new technologies into their service, and the systems office can expect to support them in the effort.

One of the earliest Internet-based technological innovations in interlibrary loan services was the Research Libraries Group's Ariel software (http://www.infotrieve.com/ariel/index.html). First introduced in the early 1990s, Ariel quickly became a standard for e-mailing and transferring printed documents online. The software scans paper resources at any resolution and then easily transmits the electronic copy to other organizations running Ariel software. The software has built in viewers and management tools to assist users in quality control and document tracking. Recent enhancements to the Ariel software allow libraries to e-mail documents directly to patrons or to store scanned documents on a Web server for patron access. Ariel reports that more than 9,000 organizations worldwide now use this technology (http://www.infotrieve.com/ariel/ariadv.html).

A variety of other tools are available to assist organizations in managing document delivery requests. Some ILS vendors have integrated document delivery management into their systems. One solution is Clio ILL Management software (http://cliosoftware.com/public). Clio offers management of both traditional paper and electronic document delivery requests. ILLiad, developed by Virginia Tech, marketed by OCLC, and supported by Atlas Systems, is another popular document delivery management package. It offers workflow management tools, generates statistics, and automatically links with OCLC's Interlibrary Loan subsystem. The systems office might be asked to assist the document delivery staff with running such servers and providing access to staff. Libraries have also developed systems to assist with increasing efficiency and reducing document delivery costs. An example of this type of solution is the RAPID Project currently being developed at Colorado State University.

11

Summary

In combination with more traditional resources, libraries must seek methods of utilizing technology that connect people to the information they seek. The information technology organization, and especially the systems librarian, must play a pivotal leadership role and offer the vision necessary to shape and promote the appropriate and effective use of technology. Technology has the potential to increase collaborative teaching and learning; collaboration is a complex and challenging process. Leaders in information technology provide the tools and develop the skills to enable effective utilization of technology.

Several myths have influenced the adoption and growth of technology. First among these is that technology saves money. The savings are really only a potential that requires an understanding of initial investments and continuing and indirect costs such as staff training, upgrades, support, and maintenance. Ideally, the benefits of both long- and short-range planning guide everyone toward an understanding of how each investment will move libraries closer to realizing their goals. For academic libraries, it would be both foolish and unrealistic to ignore the influences and benefits of information technology; technology costs should be considered as an investment, not a savings.

A second technology myth is that everyone can learn new technologies in the same way and at the same pace. Training must be available and flexible enough to address many learning styles. Most people will not, on their own initiative, adopt new technologies without some effort and encouragement; they are comfortable accomplishing their work in the old familiar ways. Change might only happen slowly and is occasionally accompanied by stress and conflict. The best managers either know instinctively or have learned certain techniques that help ease technology transitions and reduce the stress of change. Commitment to lifelong learning permeates the most effective information technology organizations. In academic libraries, this should be clearly articulated in the mission statement. An effective manager must plan to spend a significant amount of time encouraging and mentoring staff members to develop a love of learning.

Technology is a long way from being able to record and reproduce fully what happens in a face-to-face encounter. Artificial intelligence cannot yet substitute for the reference interview. Neither is information technology synonymous with knowledge. The purpose of higher education and the campus experience is complex and includes enabling knowledge acquisition as well as development of a whole range of other skills and talents, both social and intellectual.

The "digital divide" exists on campuses, but it can be subtle. Not all students and faculty are equally adept at utilizing technology. Research shows that faculty value technical help from students but that not all students completely understand all technologies. When moving forward on important decisions, consider the data, but also remember that campus culture, politics, common sense, and wise judgment have a role. Be sensitive to groups of users who may perceive themselves to be marginalized, such as adjunct faculty and distance learners.

The observations presented here might better be called "suggestions for further research" or "how to figure out which trends to watch for in the future." Making predictions about the future is a risky business, but in an information technology organization, managers must learn to anticipate changes on the horizon to be as well positioned as possible. This chapter is broadly divided into trends in technology and trends in higher education.

Trends in Technology

Various resources are available to help identify trends in new technology as they relate to libraries. Scan periodicals such as *Wired, The Internet Librarian,* or *Computers in Libraries. Syllabus: Technology for Higher Education* tracks technology in the context of the academic environment. Trade publications make controlled circulation copies available and are listed in "Resource Materials" at the end of the book. Be open to visionaries, no matter how far-fetched they may sound; a surprising number of early science fiction technology visions sound very ordinary today. For example, be aware of the work of scholars like Nicholas Negroponte and his colleagues at the MIT Media Lab.

Clearly one of the most noteworthy technology trends in the last twenty years has been the networking of computers and the integration of resources within the Web environment. The Internet has created opportunities for technological convergence. OpenURL, personalization, metasearching, and digitization are examples of technologies that would have been impossible without the Internet.

OpenURL is an evolving standard strongly supported by the library community, electronic resource publishers, producers, and vendors. This technology uses link resolver software to identify URLs that contain descriptive metadata about the content of particular Web pages. As the user searches, an OpenURL-enabled system is capable of retrieving highly relevant, context sensitive results. For example, the Colorado Alliance of Research Libraries developed and licenses Gold Rush, an OpenURL resolver marketed as a "discovery and management tool for electronic resources" (http://grweb.coalliance.org).

A promising trend in personalizing search results is the development of metasearching. Metasearch results include a wide range of formats and sources. This is accomplished through what is commonly called a "federated" search engine. Results may include images, citations, full-text documents, or other materials. These can be de-duplicated and sorted in a variety of ways. The systems office may need to do a certain amount of configuration and profiling to be able to offer a particular resource as part of a comprehensive search.

Digitization initiatives represent a logical extension of library service, making a wealth of materials more accessible than ever before and linking them through access points that enrich traditional finding tools. The trend in this area is that systems offices are assuming a growing, proactive leadership role in digital initiatives.

Developments in miniaturization are another key area to watch. There seems to be an inverse relationship between the power of technology and cost. Hardware components are getting smaller and lighter, more powerful, and less expensive. In particular, costs are declining for PDAs, making them more attractive to a broader audience. A library might use them for inventory; the public might beam citation information or due date reminders into them. Wireless capabilities are becoming commonplace. Users are beginning to expect wireless access not only on campus but also in coffee shops, hotels, and airports.

Network, or thin-client, computers are a hybrid between dumb terminals and personal computers. As with other technologies, there are associated costs and benefits to explore. They are usually limited to browser access and represent a shift to more server-side applications and a need for increased network bandwidth. Although early network computers were not wildly popular because of high cost, they may be a solution to consider in certain environments that require high performance and security with minimal maintenance. Some thin-client devices are now available for less than $500. Visit Thin Planet's Web site to learn about current trends in thin-client computing (http://www.thinplanet.com).

Other technologies are also quickly changing. Floppy disks are losing popularity as a removable storage media and are being replaced by other portable media with larger capacities such as USB keys, compact flash cards, and memory sticks. Enhanced whiteboard, or "smart" board, technology is maturing.

These devices are becoming particularly popular tools for collaborative projects. Flat-panel displays are quickly replacing CRT monitors. As technologies mature and peripheral device components shrink in size, the trend of will certainly continue for all types of computer equipment.

Avoid the temptation merely to automate the things you did manually yesterday. While efficiencies are surely gained, it is preferable, perhaps especially in an academic setting, to encourage creative thinking that utilizes technologies in ways that are transformational. As systems librarian, develop the vision to lead the organization forward in technology. Continually reevaluate work flow to take advantage of new ideas and trends.

Trends in Higher Education

Trends in higher education can be a harbinger for change in libraries. To remain viable and to keep its position as the "heart of the university," academic libraries need to proactively address the changing needs of academe. The results of a recent ERIC search on trends in higher education show a decline in male enrollment, a slight increase in doctorates awarded, new reliance on distance learning, an increase in lifelong learning, and a graying professorate. Identifying trends helps us plan and prioritize a course for future action.

Electronic resources will continue as an integral component of the library's collections. The number of resources available electronically is constantly growing and the technologies continually changing. For example, Internet2 and partner libraries are working on Shibboleth, a middleware solution that will help libraries manage authentication issues for electronic resources (http://shibboleth. internet2.edu). Systems offices will need to discover and implement tools that support electronic resources.

Collaborative campus projects will increasingly become the norm. This is an opportunity for the systems librarian to take a leadership role. Institutional repositories are an example of an emerging joint concern. Libraries and their partners (such as faculty, the graduate school, and computing services) must work together to determine the appropriate model for providing better access to and preserving the intellectual resources created on campus. Some institutions have decided to utilize solutions such as MIT's dSpace or the Berkeley Electronic Press software to manage these resources. Whatever model a campus pursues, there is some urgency to move forward before valuable resources are lost. Beyond the systems department, other library staff might play a role in organizing and managing resources. Campuses have implemented various course management or e-learning systems such as WebCT and Blackboard. Systems such as these are becoming increasingly popular to support both traditional classroom courses as well as distance learning environments. Some systems assistance with integrating library resources or services might be required for librarians or other campus faculty who use these systems.

Information technology provides abundant opportunities for leadership, collaboration, and professional development on campus. Technology management has an impact on the effectiveness of an academic library in fulfilling its mission. The systems librarian plays a pivotal role in transforming technological solutions into learning experiences.

Resource Materials

The materials in this section are intended to supplement the discussion in the text with concrete examples. The samples are not necessarily definitive but represent a starting point for local adaptation. All of these materials may be modified for use in libraries.

Account Policy

Example of a LAN Account Policy

The library utilizes a local area network (LAN) for many job-related tasks. Your LAN account will enable you to perform your job and communicate with other library employees more effectively. It also provides you with Internet access. A campus computer account application is also necessary.

Your supervisor can help you get started, or you may contact the systems librarian for help at any time. Training sessions are offered on a regular basis both within the library and from campus computer services; watch for announcements.

A secure password will be assigned to you when this application is processed; keep it confidential. The security of the entire network relies on each individual. It is expected that everyone will use his or her privileges judiciously.

Computers in the library are for library assigned tasks. Customization of library workstations is strongly discouraged; there is no guarantee that custom desktops can be preserved if they conflict with routine systems maintenance tasks. Occasionally an assigned workstation will be moved, changed, or updated by systems staff. Every effort will be made to provide advance notice of this work, but individuals are ultimately responsible for their own backups.

Installing personal software, including software downloaded from the Internet, utilizes finite computing resources inappropriately and jeopardizes the stability and security of your workstation as well as that of all networked computers in the library. It may also render the library and the university legally liable for licensing infractions. Installing software for work purposes, including software downloaded from the Internet, can also lead to problems with workstation maintenance or to license infractions. If you do install software that is not one of the standard packages supported by the systems office, please notify us within a few days and provide us with a copy of the license.

Downloading data files from remote sources that run under installed applications should not cause any system conflicts. If this type of file is obtained, 'it is generally good practice to put it into a temporary directory and check it for viruses before sharing the data or saving it to the network. Avoid using disks to move data between public use computers and office computers. Public use computers are more susceptible to viruses. Run a virus check from a staff workstation on any disk that you use to copy files from another computer.

Use of the Internet or the World Wide Web for personal purposes should be limited to personal time. Use of library equipment and supplies for accessing the Internet or the World Wide Web is generally reserved for work purposes. If there are occasional exceptions to this general rule, employees are expected to reimburse the library for any costs related to personal use of library equipment or supplies. This policy is consistent with the policy of the library on the use of any library-owned equipment or supplies.

Appropriate Use Policy

Note: Adapted from University of Colorado at Boulder Libraries policy

Computers shall include hardware, software, and access to local and remote systems including the Internet. Staff members shall include library professional and paraprofessional staff and student employees. Staff members have the responsibility to make use of the Library computers in an effective, ethical, and legal manner. Computers shall be used in a manner consistent with the objectives of the Library.

As a condition of use of the library facilities, the staff member agrees:

• to respect the intended purposes of Library computers,

• to respect the privacy of other users, and

• to respect the integrity of Library computers.

Staff members shall not intentionally seek information on, obtain copies of, or modify files, tapes, password, or any type of data belonging to other users unless specifically asked to do so.

Staff members shall not develop or execute programs that could harass other users, infiltrate computer systems, or alter software components of the system.

Software programs are protected by Section 117 of the 1976 Copyright Act. Unless they have written the program themselves, staff members do not have the right to make and distribute copies of programs without specific permissions of the copyright holder. The same holds true for copyrighted data files including but not limited to music and video files.

Staff members shall not make copies of Library-owned software unless specifically authorized to do so.

Staff members shall not load personal copies of software on Library-owned computers unless specifically authorized to do so.

Violations of these conditions may result in the suspension of computing privileges, disciplinary review, termination of employment, or legal action. The Library reserves the right to examine users' stored information when investigating cases of computing abuse.

The physical abuse of any computing equipment of supplies will be reported to the campus police and to the appropriate administrative office.

Name _____ Date _____

Department _____

Software Title Version _____

_____Original Disk/CD _____License Agreement

_____Original Manual Serial Number

I have read and understand the Library Policy on Appropriate Use of Library Computers. The software listed above is my personal copy, and I have paid all purchase or license fees for its use.

_____

Signature Date

Automation Consultants

http://www.libraryhq.com/consultants.html
http://www.tsl.state.tx.us/ld/pubs/techcons/
http://dlis.dos.state.fl.us/bld/Library_Tech/ConsultList.htm

Business Continuity Plan Questionnaire

1. Business disruptions can be caused from a wide variety of occurrences. Please indicate which, if any, of the following events have caused a disruption in your area or process's daily business. In addition, indicate the number of times this event has caused a disruption (in the last three years), the duration (on average) of the disruption, and the impact it had on your area or process (using a scale of 1–5).

Type of Disruption	Experienced ? Y or N	# of Occurrences	Duration	1 = No Impact, 5 = Severe Impact
Power Loss				
Fire				
Severe Weather				
Loss of Voice Communications				
Loss of Data Communications				
Lost/Corrupted Data				
Work Stoppage/Strike				
Water Damage				
Other				

2. Rate your area's dependency of each the following (1 = No Dependency, 5 = Extreme Dependency):

	1	2	3	4	5
Natural Gas (heat)					
Electricity					
Water					
Internet					
E-mail					
Phone					
Other					

3. Rate your area or process's **potential reliance on access to and use of** the following communications services **to implement recovery** (1 = Not Required, 5 = Extreme).

Communication Service	1	2	3	4	5
Long Distance Service					
Local Service					
Company E-mail Services					
Internet or Other Public Network					
Automated Phone Systems					
Emergency Dispatch Services					
Department's Emergency Pager					

4. Rate the **reliance of your area or process on** the following financial categories (e.g., where does funding for your area come from?) (1= Not Dependent, 5 = Extreme Dependency).

Exposure Type	1	2	3	4	5
Student Tuition					
Grants					
Donations					
Government Student Aid					
Administration					
Conference Income					
Interest Income					
Endowment					
Other					

5. Indicate the direct impact your area has on each of the following items **when your area or process is "down."** (1 = No Impact, 5 = Severe Impact)

Exposure Type	1 Day	2 Days	3–7 Days	1 Wk	2–4 Wks	> 4 Wks
Student Tuition						
Grants						
Donations						
Government Student Aid						
Administration						
Conference Income						
Interest Income						
Endowment						
Other						

6. What is the **direct impact of your area or process on the University** in the following areas **if your area or process is shut down** for the following periods of time? (1 = No Impact, 5 = Severe Impact)

	1 Day	2 Days	Days 3–7	1 Wk	2–4 Wks	> 4 Wks
Cash Flow						
Competitive Advantage						
Endowment Donations						
Financial Reporting						
Industry Image						
Employee Morale						
Customer Service						
Vendor Relations						
Regulatory						
Increase in Liability						
Other						

7. List your critical **"INTERNAL"** area/process dependencies (e.g., your dependency on other departments within the University). Rate these dependencies (1 = Little Dependency, 5 = Extreme Dependency).

Department	1	2	3	4	5

8. How long can your area operate without any of the internal departments listed above?

Department	1 Day	2 Days	Days 3–7	1 Wk	Wks 2–4	> 4 Wks

9. Which departments depend on your area or process? Rate these dependencies (1 = Little Dependency, 5 = Extreme Dependency).

Department	1	2	3	4	5

10.   How long can these departments operate without your services?

Department	1 Day	2 Days	3–7 Days	1 Wk	2–4 Wks	> 4 Wks

11.   Are there any "**EXTERNAL**" vendors or other sources not controlled by the University **on which you are dependent?** Rate these dependencies (1 = Little Dependency, 5 = Extreme Dependency).

External Dependency	1	2	3	4	5

12.   What is the duration that you can operate without these vendors' services?

External Dependency	1 Day	2 Days	Days 3–7	1 Wk	Wks 2–4	> 4 Wks

13. Are there any "**EXTERNAL**" vendors or other sources not controlled by the University who are **dependent on you?** Rate these dependencies (1 = Little Dependency, 5 = Extreme Dependency).

External Dependency	1	2	3	4	5

14. What is the duration that these vendors can operate without your area?

External Dependency	1 Day	2 Days	3–7 Days	1 Wk	2–4 Wks	> 4 Wks

15. Are you required to submit any regulatory documents (local, state, or federal)? What? When? List only most important.

Documents (indicate local, state, federal)	When?

16. Do you deposit funds directly to the bank?

Yes		No		Don't know	

17. **If not,** how does your area or process do its banking?

18. List your area's most important functions or responsibilities (primary and in general terms):

19. Do you have workaround procedures for each of these responsibilities (e.g., ways to conduct your work without a critical dependency)?

20. Do any of your business functions use special, or one-of-a-kind, software? Please rate your area or process's reliance on this software (1 = No Reliance, 5 = Extreme Reliance).

Software	Process	1	2	3	4	5

21. How long can your process function without the software listed above?

Software	1 Day	2 Days	3–7 Days	1 Wk	2–4 Wks	> 4 Wks

22. Are critical computer data stored on your department's desktops backed up?

	Yes	No	Don't Know
Network			
Hard Drive			
Tape			
Other			

23. If so, who is responsible for backing up the software? (Job title, not name)

	Yes	No	Don't Know
Network			
Hard Drive			
Tape			
Other			

24. If Campus Computing is responsible for backing up your vital records or data, do you know the name of the person responsible for your account?

	Yes	No	Don't Know
Network			
Hard Drive			
Tape			
Other			

25. How frequently is critical information backed up?

	Daily	Weekly	Monthly	Don't Know
Network				
Hard Drive				
Tape				
Other				

26. Where are the backups stored?

	On-site?	Off-site?	Don't Know
Network			
Hard Drive			
Tape			
Other			

27. Does your department have a formal "backup" policy?

Yes		No		Don't Know	

28. Is there a designated person authorized to obtain the backups from Campus Computing or another off-site storage facility? (Job title, not name)

Yes		No		Don't Know	

29. Do any of your business processes use special equipment? Rate your department's reliance (1 = No Reliance, 5 = Extreme Reliance).

Special Equipment	Process	1	2	3	4	5

30. How long could your processes function without the above listed equipment?

Special Equipment	1 Day	2 Days	3–7 Days	1 Wk	2–4 Wks	> 4 Wks

30. Do you have a "vital records retention" program?

Yes		No		Don't Know	

31. If so, where are the vital records stored?

On-Site		Off-Site		Don't Know	

34. Who has authorization to retrieve the vital records? (Job description, not name)

Yes		No		Don't Know	

35. What months of the year are the most critical to your area or process? Rate the relative importance of each month (1 = Not Critical, 5 = Critical).

Month	1	2	3	4	5
January					
February					
March					
April					
May					
June					
July					
August					
September					
October					
November					
December					

35. What week of the month is most critical to your area or process? Rate the importance (1 = Not Critical, 5 = Critical).

Week	1	2	3	4	5
1					
2					
3					
4					

36. What day (or days) of the week are the most critical to your area or process? Rate the importance (1 = Not Critical, 5 = Critical).

Day	1	2	3	4	5
Monday					
Tuesday					
Wednesday					
Thursday					
Friday					
Other					

37. What hours of the day are most critical to your area or process?

Hours	1	2	3	4	5
AM					
PM					

38. Does your department have an updated Emergency Evacuation Procedure and/or a Y2K Plan on file?

	Yes	No	Don't Know
Evacuation			
Y2K			

Computer Census Form

Example of a Pre-Installation Worksheet

To facilitate the move to your new computer, the systems department is asking for your help. Please complete as much of the information as you can on this worksheet. Systems staff will work with you to complete the rest. We can also help you get started with your new system and help you arrange for classes.

Cleaning Up Your Hard Drive

Moving to a new machine is a perfect opportunity to clean up your hard drive by removing unneeded files. If you are keeping particular files for archival purposes, you might choose to store them on a floppy, Zip disk, or CD instead of your computer's hard drive. If you are not sure about how to move or delete files, ask someone from systems to help you.

Begin looking at the word processing and spreadsheet files that you have on your computer. Delete the ones you no longer need or do not want. Using Windows Explorer, create a New Folder called "MOVEME". All files in this folder will be moved to your new computer.

Copy any files and folders that you want moved to your new computer to the MOVEME folder. *NOTE: Do not copy any executable programs into the MOVEME folder.* Your new computer will come with the latest version of software that is currently supported by the Libraries. Systems will preserve any browser bookmarks, so there is no need for you to move them.

Specifics About Your Old Machine

Computer Name Dept _____

Phone Date _____

IP address Inventory tag number _____

Network Address _____

OCLC Login and Password (if OCLC is used) _____

I use a wand or barcode reader with my old machine.   YES / NO

I have a printer. YES / NO If yes, brand and model: _____

_____

I share a printer with other users on a network?   YES / NO

List all IP addresses or print servers used _____

_____

Number on the wall jack that your computer is plugged into: _____

_____

Hub Brand/Serial No. (if not plugged directly into a wall jack): _____

_____

E-Mail

I currently use Outlook to read my e-mail: ☐ yes ☐ no

My campus e-mail address is _____

I have folders in my campus e-mail account that I need to have downloaded:

☐ yes ☐ no

Software

Define your currently supported applications in this section. You may be able to offer support for certain specialized software. If so, outline licensing and purchasing procedures.

Computer Equipment Replacement Plan

Background

Information technology has become an integral part of practically every task performed in the University Libraries. To remain a leader in providing IT-rich library resources, the Libraries must dedicate significant recourses to replace aging workstations. The general rule of thumb is that computers have a three- to five-year life span. Many variables affect the life span, or usefulness, of a given computer:

- Is the computer in a public area or at a staff member's desk?

- What applications are run on the computer?

- Is the computer a server?

- How quickly do software applications change for given tasks?

- Do other users share the computer via the network?

It is not cost-effective for the systems department to repair machines greater than five years old. Downstreaming machines older than three years old is not cost-effective and defeats the purpose of replacement. The time has come to manage replacement in a coordinated fashion. A replacement cycle of four years is recommended as a starting point.

Funding Sources

Funding for replacement computer equipment comes from four primary sources:

- Libraries Computer Equipment Replacement Fund

- Student Computing Fee

- Campus Faculty Computer Replacement Program

- Libraries Capital Equipment Budget

This document describes how replacement funds from each of these sources will be applied.

Libraries Computer Equipment Replacement Fund

Background

The systems librarian based on the following guidelines will manage it.

Types of Equipment

All computer equipment and peripherals. First preference will be given to staff workstations because this is a primary replacement fund for machine of this type. Second preference is to network servers. Third preference to public workstations (WebPAC or CD-ROM/network stations).

Guidelines

First preference will be given to staff workstations because this is a primary replacement fund for machine of this type. Second preference is to network servers. Third preference is to public workstations (WebPAC or CD-ROM/network stations). Although first preference is to be given to staff workstations, a percentage of this fund (15% to 20%) should be devoted to replacing servers. A small percentage should also be reserved for emergency replacement issues.

Campus Student Computing Fee (SCF) Funding

Background

A campus committee allocates the funds collected by the Student Computing Fee. The Libraries receives approximately [amount] annually. The systems librarian is the Libraries' representative on the SCF committee.

Types of Equipment

Equipment funded from this source is intended for student use. In the Libraries, this primarily includes instructional computers (for example, computers and projectors in classrooms or individual workstations in the Learning Lab) and public WebPAC and CD-ROM/network stations.

Guidelines

The goal is to replace all public machines over a three-year period. The systems department will develop a replacement schedule based on the Libraries' current inventory.

Campus Faculty Computer Replacement Program

Background

The campus set up this fund in FY 98/99. It is intended to assist schools and colleges in replacing faculty computers on a three- or four-year cycle.

Types of Equipment

Desktop and laptop computers. The Libraries' opted to support desktop computers only in the first cycle of this program because of the age of existing machines.

Guidelines

This fund is dispersed in a very defined fashion. See Web site.

Libraries Capital Equipment Budget

Background

This was traditionally the only fund used for purchase of computer equipment. In addition, this fund must support all other Libraries capital equipment needs (chairs, desks, media equipment, etc.). The fund is generally split between the Libraries' divisions.

Types of Equipment

All capital equipment. New (additional) workstations.

Guidelines

Departments that are requesting new (additional) workstation should submit requests through their division' s capital equipment process. Replacement machines will be purchased through the replacement fund, SCF funds, or faculty computer program. If a division does not need additional workstations or does not spend their entire portion of this fund, the Associate Director may use this fund to supplant replacement machines. In that case, machines will still be replaced according to the replacement schedule developed by the systems department.

Controlled Circulation Publication List

Controlled circulation publications are usually available free of charge. The qualifying basis is usually your professional purchasing power. Many of these are available in both online and hard copy. Increasingly, electronic subscriptions are preferred. Subscribing electronically often means unsolicited e-mail from advertisers that subsidize these publications.

Call Center Magazine
CIO
Communications Solutions
DB2
ENT
eWeek
InformationWeek
InfoWorld
Intelligent Enterprise
KM World
Knowledge Management
NASPA Technical Support
Network Computing

Network Magazine
Network World
New Architect
Oracle Magazine
Presentations
Small Business Computing
Software Magazine
Syllabus
Technology and Learning
Teradata Review
T.H.E. Journal
Transform Magazine
Web Design and Review

Decision-making Model

The following is an example of an organizational decision-making document in which there may be several task units within each team. It helps to define team boundaries and assigns decision making responsibilities.

Unit supervisors make the following decisions independently:

1. Hiring, proposing job descriptions, annual performance appraisals, guiding departmental workflow

2. Work assignments among members of the unit

Disciplinary actions outside the annual performance appraisal process, in consultation with the Director's Office

Facilitators, also called Team Leaders, take issues like these to their teams:

1. Changes in work assignments among members of the unit that affect the whole team

2. Problems related to staffing levels and work flow

3. Issues related to projects impacting more than one unit within the team

4. Policy questions for clarification

5. Policy proposals to gather support for further review

6. Equipment requests

Unit supervisors take issues like these to the Director or a personnel librarian:

1. Human resources problems or questions, performance issues (positive or negative)

2. Advice on priorities or decision-making process

3. Emergency budget requests

Unit supervisors work with the unit to decide:

1. Work flow issues related only to the unit

2. Procedural changes

3. Preparation of policy proposals for further review

Teams decide:

1. Work flow issues that affect more than one unit within the team

2. Staffing solutions not affecting other units or teams

3. Proposal preparation for further review

Teams get input from other teams:

1. Issues that affect other teams

2. Proposals that could be strengthened with advice or input from other teams

3. Policy issues affecting other teams or units. Discussions should include major stakeholders.

Teams take issues like these to the Policy Board or the Director's administrative group:

1. Issues which affect other teams or units

2. Issues with librarywide impact

3. Policy matters of any kind

4. When user feedback would help predict desirability of a plan or proposal

5. Proposals or projects needing librarywide feedback or a librarywide viewpoint

6. Proposals or projects with a budgetary impact

The Policy Board decides issues like these:

1. Matters brought forward from teams

2. Matters raised by Associate Directors

3. Some matters raised by the Director from outside groups or individuals

4. Matters raised by the Staff Board

The Director decides issues like these with Policy Board input:

1. Operating budget matters such as equipment/supplies, projects

2. Collection budget matters

3. Issues raised by individuals or groups external to the library

The Director decides questions like these without review:

1. Personnel matters, including merit/salary and other salary/wage budget matters with input from supervisors where appropriate. Certain personnel matters related to the faculty are decided by relevant faculty governance documents

2. Certain matters brought by outside groups or individuals:

ILS Vendor Information

The first April issue of *Library Journal* reviews the state of the integrated library systems market place each year. Vendors targeting academic libraries include the following:

- **Dynix (Horizon)** http://www.dynix.com
- **Endeavor (Voyager)** http://www.endinfosys.com
- **ExLibris (Aleph 500)** http://www.exlibris-usa.com
- **Innovative Interfaces (Millennium)** http://www.iii.com
- **Sirsi (Unicorn)** http://www.sirsi.com
- **VTLS (Virtua)** http://www.vtls.com

Job Description Form

JOB TITLE: Position #

Exempt (Y/N): HIRING RANGE:
DIVISION: DEPARTMENT:
PREPARED BY: DATE:
APPROVED BY: DATE:

SUMMARY:

ESSENTIAL DUTIES AND RESPONSIBILITIES include the following. Other duties as assigned.

- Hardware Support

- Software Support

- Networking Support

- Statistics and Use Data Management

- Help Desk and Documentation Support

QUALIFICATION REQUIREMENTS: To perform this job successfully, an individual must be able to perform each essential duty satisfactorily. The requirements listed below are representative of the knowledge, skill, and/or ability required. Reasonable accommodations may be made to enable individuals with disabilities to perform the essential functions.

EDUCATION and/or EXPERIENCE:
   Required:
   Preferred:
LANGUAGE SKILLS:
MATHEMATICAL SKILLS:
REASONING ABILITY:
OTHER SKILLS and ABILITIES:

PHYSICAL DEMANDS: The physical demands described here are representative of those that must be met by an employee to successfully perform the essential functions of this job. Reasonable accommodations may be made to enable individuals with disabilities to perform the essential functions.

WORK ENVIRONMENT: The work environment characteristics described here are representative of those an employee encounters while performing the essential functions of this job. Reasonable accommodations may be made to enable individuals with disabilities to perform the essential functions.

Job Evaluation Form

Performance Review and Development System

Name: _____ ID Number: _____

Position: _____ Department: _____

Hire Date: _____ Review Period: _____

Reviewed by: _____ Ext.: _____

General Directions:

The employee and the manager have an equal responsibility to contribute to the information contained in this review. Both shall agree on the job responsibilities, job goals, and the related standards against which actual performance will be compared. The completion of this document will be the result of a review discussion between the employee and the supervisor on its contents. The review can be typed or handwritten.

Overall Performance Measurement Explanation:

NI NEEDS IMPROVEMENT—Has not met agreed-to objectives. Requires improvement in performance to be a positive contributor to the University.

PC Demonstrates a POSITIVE CONTRIBUTION to the University— Is a valued member of the team and the organization who achieved agreed-to objectives, fulfilled the responsibilities of the job, whose hard work and effort is evident, and who is fully involved in the activities of the job.

EP Demonstrates EXCEPTIONAL PERFORMANCE—In addition to making a positive contribution to the University, as defined above, consistently exceeds agreed-to objectives and the responsibilities of the job in a way which has a significant, positive impact on the quality of the University's strategic plan, systems, and way of doing business.

NE NOT EVALUATED—May be applicable to a particular job duty/responsibility or job goal, but must not be used as an overall measurement. If used in measurement a particular job duty/responsibility or job goal, this type of measurement must be explained by the measurement manager.

Essential Duties and Responsibilities From current job description, list key responsibilities that will be evaluated this review period.	Performance Standards For each duty and/or responsibility selected for review, list the performance standard, which tells how well the duty and/or responsibility is to be performed.	Actual Performance Give a brief, representative description of the employee's actual performance during the review period.	Measurement Using the scale provided, compare performance to standards set.			
			NI	PC	EP	NE

Job Goals Goals to be accomplished during this review period.	Goal Standards For each goal list the performance standards, which tells how well the goal is to be performed.	Actual Performance Give a brief, representative description of the employee's actual performance on goals set during the review period.	Measurement Using the scale provided, compare performance to standards set.			
			NI	PC	EP	NE

Improvement Plan(s)

For any NI (needs improvement) measurement given, describe what will be done to improve performance, the date(s) the improvement is due, and who will be involved.

Plan	Due Date	Responsible Person

Development Plan(s)

Describe what will be done to help the employee pursue his/her own career goals. Include the date(s), action, and who will be involved.

Plan	Due Date	Responsible Person

Overall Measurement and Narrative Comments

Measurement: PC EP NI

Descriptive/Narrative Comments:

Employee's Signature: _____   Date: _____

By signing this form, employee verifies receipt only, not whether employee agrees/disagrees with this review.

Supervisor's Signature: _____   Date: _____

Supervisor's Superior's Signature: _____   Date: _____

Signature is required on all overall measurements of "EP" and "NI"

Employee's Comments to Overall Measurement (optional)

Library Technology Plan

(This is a model based on a draft plan produced by the University of Colorado at Boulder Libraries. The authors would like acknowledge that this was a collaborative project with contributions from numerous individuals in the Libraries and on campus.)

Libraries are highly affected by the networked information technology revolution. The traditional role of the library takes new forms as technological changes continue to transform the academic enterprise. Libraries respond to these transformations through a rigorous planning process and wise reinvestment of limited resources. This plan addresses four major areas of planning activity:

I. Electronic Content Acquisition

The library has been at the center of the explosion of electronic information. The first purchases of electronic products cost [amount]. Expenditures for electronic resources have now risen to over [amount]. A wide range of intellectual content is currently acquired primarily via access to remote databases, specialized web research tools, and electronic document delivery all of which remain available 24 hours a day, 7 days a week because it is our goal to provide users with intellectual resources independent of time or place. This encompasses both intellectual content, such as full text electronic journals and books, as well as resources that index discipline-specific or general print collections, such as FirstSearch or the catalog. While we purchase some full-text journals through direct subscriptions or one-time expenditures, more frequently we purchase them through cooperative or package licensing agreements. Consequently, it is our intent to pursue the acquisition and retrospective conversion of electronic resources.

Participants:

• Bibliographers

• Consortia partners

• Database and other information vendors

• Campus IT Professionals

Expected Costs:

• Annual operating cost: [amount]

• Expect an increase of 7% to 10% per year for new purchases and inflation

• Personnel

Existing Expenditures:

- Annual operating cost: Computer files (CD-ROM) [amount]
- Electronic journals [amount]
- Bibliographic utilities [amount]

Funding:

- Electronic resources are primarily funded by reallocation and reinvestment through the materials budget. Although wise and careful group purchasing stretches these funds, our ability to maintain and grow the current number of electronic resources is deteriorating. Shrinking increases to the materials budget is threatening acquisitions in general and electronic subscriptions as part of that. If annual increases remain at this level the continued expansion of electronic resources is certain to be compromised. Reduction or elimination of any of the outside funding sources will also seriously affect purchases of electronic resources.
- The budget request indicates a need for an additional [amount] annually as an inflation fighter.

Timing:

- Electronic content acquisition is a central priority. During the next three to five years, it is critical that the library continually assess the electronic information market in relation to the sources of ongoing funding.

II. Electronic Content Creation

The library creates electronic content in two ways: by providing item descriptions for the online catalog and by digitizing collections and creating metadata-level descriptions for those collections.

A. Descriptive, Item-Based Cataloging

The catalog is the first recourse for most users searching for information in the collections. The staff creates descriptive cataloging for every new item purchased, regardless of format. Either a copy cataloging provider sells the records to us, or they are created as original cataloging. Although cataloging is available for the majority of new and recent acquisitions, complete descriptions for many items purchased before 1970 are not in the catalog. For these items we need to create machine-readable descriptive records. Older items are vital to the research conducted by students and faculty so it is crucial to create records for these holdings. Finally, many of these items are unique, not owned by another library in the state or region.

Many libraries are now outsourcing portions of their cataloging. Outsourcing is an attractive option because it redeployment of personnel funding into other services. Cataloging is a precise intellectual activity based on national standards. Some outsourcing provides inconsistent results such as improper application of national standards or local policies. Nevertheless the Library must evaluate outsourcing to position ourselves for the future.

Participants:

- Technical processing personnel
- Outsourcing vendors

Expected Costs:

- The total cost to complete retrospective cataloging is estimated to be [amount]. The budget request asks the university to fund [amount] annually for 3 years; the library will contribute [amount] annually for three years. The second phase of this effort is planned for next year. The budget request also includes a new faculty line to coordinate electronic collection development activities.

Existing Expenditures:

- Current cataloging is supported through salaries at a rate of approximately [amount] annually for both print and electronic resources.

Funding:

- During phase one, partially from the university and partially through library salary savings by leaving traditional print cataloging vacancies empty for a period of three years.

Timing:

- This would begin with converting small collections this year with full-scale record creation beginning next year.

B. Creating Digital Collections

Digitizing is an option for unique collections. By creating digital images of collections such as manuscripts or sheet music, we provide a new means of access to users and preserve the collection at the same time. A vital component of digital collections is the metadata description of items in those collections; metadata descriptions allow enhanced search retrieval for the digital items users require for research. The metadata creation process is comparable to cataloging traditional print materials and requires significant involvement of trained personnel.

Several faculty members are taking a lead role in digitization projects. The projects include collaboration with archives, historical societies, libraries, and museums. Participants create a digital library-museum that provides access to the rich historical and cultural resources of this state. A pilot project to create a digital collection of sheet music is now underway.

The impact and use of digital collections is expected to grow in the near future. Faster home Internet connections and other network enhancements proposed by initiatives such as Internet2 will make is easier for users to access these collections from any location. The development of digital collections will enhance the current and future outreach activities of the faculty while increasing our capacity as a research resource.

Participants:

- Library personnel

- Partners in the Colorado Digitization Project

- Campus IT Professionals

Expected Costs:

- The pilot project had an approximate startup cost of [amount]. Most of this budget was dedicated to purchasing scanning equipment; minimal personnel costs were included. Reallocating duties of existing staff will complete the majority of the work for this project.

Existing Expenditures:

- The library funded the [amount] startup costs for the pilot. The library will also receive a [amount] grant as a partner.

Funding:

- Funding for future digitization projects will be generated through reallocation and reinvestment; R & D funds will also be sought via other funding agencies.

Funding and Timing:

- This would begin, based upon funding, in the next academic year.

III. Shared IT Infrastructure Services

The success of any of the above activities requires a strong campus IT infrastructure. The library is both a supplier and a user of that infrastructure, providing user support and facilities, as well as utilizing campus and external networks and middleware services. Investments in each of these areas will be needed on an ongoing basis. In general, the needs in each of these areas will be congruent with broad campus requirements, but on occasion the scholarly support mission of the library may necessitate accelerated development.

A. User support

User support is divided into two areas in the library: instructional support and back office support. The systems department supports all of these activities.

1. Instructional Support

The library faculty is highly engaged in teaching across all disciplines. The library teaches students how to think critically about and use the ever-growing body of information both in electronic and print formats. The plethora of information now available on the web has accelerated the need for students to apply critical thinking skills when evaluating information; critical evaluation of information is one of the key concepts taught in every library instruction session. The library provides an active learning environment in its electronic classroom. This single classroom is consistently overbooked thus making it essential to expand the hands-on teaching facilities in the library. In the future, the library will need to support innovative and new teaching and learning environments. For example, the program plan for the new branch library calls for virtual reality learning environments, such as CAVES.

Besides classroom teaching, the library offers just-in-time instruction at reference and information desks. These locations must also be equipped with appropriate equipment, software, and networking capacity. Last year nearly [number] reference questions were answered at the reference desks.

2. Back Office Support

The behind-the-scenes work of the library is equally important in order for direct instruction to occur. More than [number] FTE staff work in non-public areas. It is here where the library acquires, organizes, and prepares print and electronic materials for users. The systems department handles administrative support for library faculty and staff machines. While the campus provides funds to address replacement of faculty and public machines, the library has initiated a replacement plan for staff machines.

3. Information Technology Support

The systems department maintains the library IT infrastructure. The department is responsible for the catalog, servers, desktop workstations and network printers, as well as associated peripherals in the main library, the branch libraries, and the off-site storage facility. While the department's responsibility stops at the b-jack, there is considerable campus cooperation to ensure network access for each of these machines.

The systems staff of [number] FTE has reached its limit in supporting these services. To maintain current levels of service, the department needs at least [number] additional FTE. However, future developments (such as the proposed branch library) indicate that the department will need [number] additional FTE in the IT Professional classification over the next five years.

Training is a growing concern for the systems department. Currently, the department works with the library's Faculty/Staff Development Committee to offer basic skills training such as Windows and word processing. Advanced training is also conducted for catalog system modules or software packages specific to the library (such as Passport for Windows). When specialized needs arise, training is sought from other sources. Because of the unique relationship of basic skill and library-specific training conducted, an additional faculty line is recommended to coordinate this training library-wide. Peer institutions have begun to implement this model.

Participants:

• Systems department

• ITS professionals

Expected Costs:

• The systems department requires an additional [number] FTE IT Professional I and [number] FTE IT Technician IIs in order to maintain current systems and deploy new technologies. [amount]

Existing Expenditures:

• Operations hardware & software [amount]

• Document delivery [amount]

• Systems personnel [amount]

Funding:

• No internal funds are available for these positions.

Timing:

• This request is part of the annual budget request.

B. Commons

In addition to the instructional activities described above, the library plays an essential role in the provision of access to the broad student population. The fit is natural: the library has long been the physical center of academic activity; the extended operational hours provide maximum access; and the availability of user support facilities provide maximum efficiency. Even with the increase of student ownership of computers, use of the commons continues unabated, due to support and printing capabilities.

Maintaining standard facilities (e.g. catalog kiosks and other network stations to access bibliographic and full-text information via the Web or CD-ROM) in the library will require periodic hardware and software upgrades and expansions. The regular budget process provides only partial funding. In the past academic year, the library embarked on a project to provide technology team rooms.

These facilities, based on the team rooms in other parts of campus, offer students an opportunity to use current technologies such as electronic white boards, scanners, and projectors in a collaborative environment. The library and the campus computing center jointly support these rooms and provide a model for future cooperation between the units. Future joint projects will address issues such as electronic printing management to better control the explosion of printing in public areas, and the exploration of production software, e.g. html editors, on the equipment in the team room environment.

Participants:

- Campus computing center
- Budget committee
- IT council

Expected Costs:

- Annual operating cost
- Personnel

Existing Expenditures:

- Equipment renewal and replacement
- Personnel

Funding:

- The library relies on funding at the current level to continue services. This funding builds a three-year replacement cycle for all computers. We requested an additional [amount] to help achieve this goal.

Timing:

- Facilities are reviewed on an annual basis.

C. Networking

In their role of support for electronic collaboration and information, the library has become a highly demanding consumer of advanced networking services. The requirements for networking are of several types:

Ubiquitous access—patrons throughout the library need reasonable performance connectivity. This applies to workstations within the library and placement of network ports for personal laptops.

Untethered access—successful initiatives have demonstrated the value of wireless connectivity. The ability of a researcher or student to take notes from any carrel or within the stacks represents a marked increase in productivity. Provisioning of the service can take several forms, ranging from purchase of wireless cards by individuals to programs that loan out either cards or laptops with cards installed.

High-performance access—several of the service offerings described earlier in this document necessitate higher performance access. Servers for electronic content need to be placed on well-located, fast links in order to handle the anticipated load. Advanced collaborative environments will need specialized QoS capacities in order to sustain their video and interactive components. Such QoS requirements may be met by over provisioning within the campus network, but will likely require special handling at the campus egress to insure good performance in the external networked arena.

Participants:

- ITS and the IT Council—for campus networking issues

- I2—for external access

Expected Costs:

- One time capitalization

- Annual operating cost

- Personnel

Existing Expenditures:

- Switch, access point, and cable maintenance

Funding:

- Timing:

D. Middleware

As libraries move into electronic services, they place new and important demands on higher-level network services. Authentication of users must shift from a location-based mechanism to an association-based mechanism. Similarly, other attributes of users must be stored electronically in directories to control more refined aspects of access. Moreover, licensing structures will become more sophisticated, with usage of ubiquitous resources connected more closely to particular campus communities. The development of campus-wide authorization services will be needed to support such economic arrangements.

These developments will likely be lead by innovative projects between regional or national associations of universities on one side and progressive publishers on the other. Once the protocols are established, it is anticipated that such access alternatives will spread rapidly, and we will want to implement such schema.

Participants:

- IT Council
- ITS
- CNI
- I2

Expected Costs:

- One-time capitalization
- Annual operating cost
- Personnel

Existing Expenditures:

- The campus currently does not have a middleware infrastructure
- Funding
- Timing

IV. Scholarly Collaboration

Through traditional collections of serials and monographs, libraries have historically been the major facilities supporting scholarly collaboration. As we move into the electronic era of ubiquitous information and advanced collaboration, this role will likely persist, through both the provision of user support for distributed users and the provision of centralized access and support centers.

Appendices

Appendices may include supplementary materials such as budget request, project plans, or replacement plans.

Online Help Page

Top of Form

Libraries Systems Help Page

Name of Submitter	
Name of User (if different)	
Department	
Email address	
Subject	
Description of issue	
Tag number	(If multiple machines, use comma to separate)
	(Six digit number on a yellow tag)

Bottom of Form

Password Policy and Instructions

Because of some recent security concerns with library computers, the systems office is establishing network and system policies that will require everyone to change passwords on a regular basis. This will affect your desktop workstation as well as some services to which you connect.

Campus policy recommends that passwords must include a mix of character classes (lowercase letter, uppercase letter, number, punctuation, etc.) and contain six or more characters. Passwords must not contain:

- A single word that can be found in the common English dictionary in any form, even with an uppercase letter in the middle (window, tree, treetop would all fail)

- Your personal name, common names, or log-name (i.e., john, jonathan)

- Proper nouns, including geographic locations (i.e., Colorado, Mongolia)

- Three or more consecutive repeated characters (e.g., "aaa" would fail)

Passwords should not be stored on Post-It notes stuck to computer monitors.

Effective January 1, your workstations will require you to change your Windows password as you log on. After that, you will be prompted to change your password every six months unless you've already changed it.

Steps to Change Windows Log-on Password

Note: The procedure for changing the computer log on password is the same for all Microsoft operating systems (NT, Win2000, XP).

1. While you are logged on to your computer, press the following three keys at the same time: "Ctrl-Alt-Delete".

2. A Windows Security window will pop up showing six buttons. The first button on the bottom row is "Change Password." Click on it. Another window will open showing the current username and domain, with 3 blank fields. Enter your old password (the password you currently use to log on to your computer), a new password and confirmation of the new password in the boxes and press OK. The system will respond with the message "Your password has been changed."

3. The next time you log on to your computer use the new password.

Professional Reading

You will never have the time to do enough professional reading. This is a selected list of titles that you may scan and find useful. Sometimes your Serials Department will route newly received issues to you on request. Ingenta (formerly UnCover Reveal) provides an alerting service that will e-mail tables of contents of current issues. See http://www.ingenta.com. The Informed Librarian is another table of contents service. It's free from http://www.infosourcespub.com/index.cfm. The service provides a list of links to tables of contents, sometimes with free full text, for many library-related publications, including technical titles like Byte, Computers in Libraries, D-Lib, and Library Hi Tech.

Advanced Technology Libraries
American Libraries
Annual Review of Information Science and Technology
Charleston Advisor
Chronicle of Higher Education
College & Research Libraries
College & Research Libraries News
Computers in Libraries
D-Lib Magazine
Educause Review
Electronic Library
Feliciter (CANADA)
Information Technology and Libraries (ITAL)
Information Today
Journal of Academic Librarianship
Journal of the American Society for Information Science
LASIE (Australia)
Library Computing
Library Futures Quarterly
Library Hi Tech
Library Hi Tech News
Library Journal
Library Systems Newsletter
Library Technology Reports
Library Trends
http://LISNews.com
Online
Program (UK)
RLG DigiNews
VINE (UK)

Selected Acronyms

An up-to-date computer dictionary is an essential reference tool. We include a citation to Hodges 1999 volume, *Computers: Systems, Terms and Acronyms* in the Reference list. There are also online computer glossaries available at Computeruser.com (http://www.computeruser.com/resources/dictionary/ dictionary.html), Webopedia (http://www.webopedia.com), and InstantWeb (http://www.InstantWeb.com/foldoc/foldoc.cgi?Free+On-line+Dictionary).

ANSI—American National Standards Institute

API—application programming interface

Blog—Web log

COA—Committee on Accreditation, American Library Association

DHCP—dynamic host configuration protocol

DNS—domain name service

DSL—digital subscriber line

EAD—encoded archival description

EDI—electronic data interchange

ERIC—Educational Resources Information Center

FAQ—frequently asked question

FTP—File Transfer Protocol

IEEE—Institute of Electronic and Electrical Engineers

IFB—invitation for bid

ILS—integrated library system

IMLS—Institute for Museum and Library Services

IT—information technology

ISO—International Standards Organization

KVM—keyboard, video, mouse

LAN—local area network

LSP—Linked Systems Project

LSTA—Library Services and Technology Act

MARC—Machine-readable cataloging

MLS—Master of Library Science

netBIOS—network basic input-output system

NISO—National Information Standards Organization

NREN—National Research and Education Network

NSF—National Science Foundation

OSI—Open Systems Interconnection

PDA—personal digital assistant

PERT—program evaluation and review technique

RFI—request for information

RFID—radio frequency identification

RFP—request for proposal

RFQ—request for quotation

SMTP—simple mail transfer protocol

SNMP—simple network management protocol

SQL—structured query language

TCP/IP—transmission control protocol/Internet protocol

Telnet—terminal emulation link network

WAN—wide area network

Server Configuration Reference Sheet

		Notes
NetBios Name	Comp1	
DNS Names	www.comp1.edu	Aliases: library.edu, www.edu, www.library.edu
	www.comp1a.edu	
	www.comp1b.edu	
Domain Role	Member Server	
OS	Win2K SP 4	
Function	Website server	
	Public desktops and start menu storage	
	Tape backup device	Backup for Comp1, Comp2, Comp3
IP Addresses	X.X.X.175	Local Area Connection 2, Dual Port Server Adapter
	X.X.X.176	Local Area Connection 3, Dual Port Server Adapter #2 Disabled
	X.X.X.177	Local Area Connection, PCI Ethernet Adapter, used for library.du.edu.BETA site (legacy)
Shares	\public	E:\public
	\multimedia	E:\New Folder
	\library training	E:\public\library\library training
	\weblogs	E:\weblogs
Open Ports	25 (SMTP) 80 (HTTP) 1433 (SQL)	On X.X.X.73
	None	On X.X.X.176 Disabled
	25 (SMTP) 80 (HTTP) 1433 (SQL)	On X.X.X.177
Programs and Services	Cold Fusion	
	IIS 5.0 (WWW, SMTP)	
	Java Web Start	Legacy from temporary ILLiad
	JRE	Legacy from temporary ILLiad
	SQL Server and Mirror source	
	NetMeeting	
	Terminal Server	

Supported Software Policy

The campus adopted a standard set of supported software effective July 1, 2000, to preserve and maximize the usability and supportability of the hardware and software that is already widely used on campus. The library systems office has developed a similar set of supported software. By standardizing the software packages used in the library, the systems office can make best use of staff and student time and ensure that all users have a reliable and consistent source of support. Rapid technological change means hardware, software, and even operating systems change quickly. Manufacturers release new processor chips every three to four months. Most reports indicate that desktop hardware has a useful lifespan averaging three years. Because of this, software versions can be effectively supported for about two years after their release.

Therefore, the systems office supports most of the software packages that are supported by the campus technology services. Selected library application specific software packages (such as Passport for Windows) will also be supported by the systems office. In some cases, the library might select one specific software product to support for an entire category (i.e., Microsoft Word is the only word processing package supported). The list below indicates the current list of campus- and library-supported software packages.

Sample list:

• Office Applications: Microsoft Office XP and above

• E-Mail Reader: Eudora 3.x and above

• Outlook 2000 and above

• Library Specific Software OCLC Passport for Windows

• OCLC CatME

Web Site URLs

ACRL
   http://www.ala.org/acrl/

AntiVirus
   http://www.mcafee.com/, http://www.symantec.com/
   http://www.sophos.com/

ARL
   http://www.arl.org/

Dictionaries
   http://www.computeruser.com/resources/dictionary/dictionary.html,
   http://www.InstantWeb.com/foldoc/foldoc.cgi?Free+On-line+
   Dictionary

Digital Copyright
   http://www.umuc.edu/distance/odell/cip/listserv.html

Digital Libraries List (Diglib)
   http://infoserv.inist.fr/wwsympa.fcgi

Educause
   http://www.educause.edu/

Ergonomics
   http://www.osha.gov/SLTC/etools/computerworkstations/index.html
   http://www.tifaq.com/furniture.html

Heads of Library Technology Interest Group
   http://listserv.temple.edu/archives/holt-l.html

Internet library for librarians
   http://www.itcompany.com/inforetriever/

Knowledge Enterprise Special Interest Group (KESIG)
   http://www.sun.com/products-n-solutions/edu/commofinterest/
   elearning/sig/

Libnt-l
   http://listserv.utk.edu/archives/libnt-l.html

Library Automation Toolkit (ACLIN)
   http://www.cde.state.co.us/cdelib/technology/atauto.htm

Microsoft TechNet
   http://www.microsoft.com/technet/treeview/default.asp?url=/technet/
   security/current.asp

Nettrain
   http://listserv.acsu.buffalo.edu/archives/nettrain.html

Oss4lib-discuss
  http://lists.sourceforge.net/lists/listinfo/oss4lib-discuss

Pacs-l
  http://info.lib.uh.edu/pacsl.html

Plugins
  http://home.netscape.com/plugins/index.html

SDI services
  http://www.ingenta.com

Security
  http://www.infosyssec.org/infosyssec/
  http://www.microsoft.com/windows/ieak/en
  http://www.ciac.org/ciac/
  http://www.cert.org/
  http://hoaxbusters.ciac.org/

Systems Librarians list (Syslib-l)
  http://listserv.acsu.buffalo.edu/archives/syslib-l.html

Teaching, Learning, and Technology (TLT-SWG)
  http://listserv.nd.edu/archives/tlt-swg.html

Web4lib list
  http://sunsite.berkeley.edu/Web4Lib

Wireless Librarian
  http://people.morrisville.edu/~drewwe/wireless/

References

Barber, D. (1996). Building a digital library: Concepts and issues. *Library Technology Reports, 32*(5), (September/October): 711–714.

Barclay, D. (2000). *Managing public access computers.* New York: Neal-Schuman.

Bishoff, L., & Allen, N. (2004). *Business planning for cultural heritage institutions.* Washington, DC: Council on Library and Information Resources.

Boss, R. W. (1997). *Library administrator's automation handbook.* Medford, NJ: Information Today.

Branse, Y., Elliott, V., & Pin, L. (1996). Libraries on the web. *Electronic Library, 14*(2), (April): 117–121.

Breeding, M. (2004, January/February). Integrated library software: A guide to multiuser, multifunction systems. *Library Technology Reports, 40*(1).

Brown, J. (1988). Measuring system performance. *Information Technology and Libraries, 7,* 184–185.

Buildings, books, and bytes: Libraries and communities in the digital age. (1996). Washington, DC: Benton Foundation. Also available online at http://www.benton.org/publibrary/kellogg/buildings.html (retrieved February 25, 2004).

Chu, F. T. (1990). Evaluating the skills of the systems librarian. *Journal of Library Administration, 12,* 91–102.

Connell, T. H., & Franklin C. (1994). The Internet: Educational issues. *Library Trends, 42*(4), (spring): 608–625.

Corbly, J. E. (1997, December). Upgrading application software: Problems and perspectives. *Information Technology and Libraries, 16*(4), 193–196.

Cortez, E. M. (1987). *Proposals and contracts for library automation: Guidelines for preparing RFP's.* Chicago: ALA.

Croneis, K. S., & Henderson, P. (2002). Electronic and digital librarian positions: A content analysis of announcements from 1990 through 2000. *Journal of Academic Librarianship, 28,* 232–237.

Cronin, M. J. (1989). The second time around: Transition to a new integrated library system. In S. Glogoff (Ed.), Staff training in the automated library environment: A symposium. *Library Hi Tech, 7,* 76–77.

De Klerk, A., & Euster, J. R. (1989, spring). Technology and organizational metamorphoses. *Library Trends, 37,* 457–468.

Directory of Computer and High Technology Grants (1991–). Loxahatchee, FL: Research Grant Guides.

Dougherty, R. M. (1989). Recruiting and developing human resources to manage in a technological environment. In W. Miller (Ed.), Developing managerial competence for library automation [special issue]. *Library Hi Tech, 7,* 103–112.

Dunsire, G. (1994). A life in the week…. In G. Muirhead (Ed.), *The systems librarian: The role of the library systems manager.* London: Library Association.

Dvorak, J. C. (1995, April 25). The case for new equipment. *PC Magazine,* 89.

Epstein, S. B., & Freeman, G. (1991, June 15). Administrators of automated systems: A survey. *Library Journal, 116,* 56–57.

Eustis, J. D., & Kenney, D. J. (Compilers). (1996). *Library reorganization & restructuring* (SPEC kit 215). Washington, DC: Association of Research Libraries, Office of Management Studies.

Foote, M. (1997, November). The systems librarian in US academic libraries: A survey of announcements from College & Research Libraries News. *College & Research Libraries, 58,* 517–526.

Gilbert, S. W. (2001, October 4). Why bother? Available online at http://www.tltgroup.org/gilbert/WhyBotherLIST.htm.

Glogoff, S. (Ed.). (1989). Staff training in the automated library environment: A symposium. *Library Hi Tech, 7,* 61–83.

Gordon, B. (1996). Java: a new brew for educators, administrators, and students. *Educom Review, 31,* 44–46. Retrieved from http://www.educause.edu/asp/doclib/abstract.asp?ID=ERM9627.

Gordon, R. S. (2003). *Accidental systems librarian.* Medford, NJ: Information Today.

Gordon, R. S. (2001, November/December). A course in accidental systems librarianship. *Computers in Libraries,* 24–28.

Gorman, M. (2003). *Enduring library*. Chicago: American Library Association.

Gorman, M. (1987). The organization of academic libraries in light of automation. In J. A. Hewitt (Ed.), *Advances in library automation and networking* (Vol. 1, pp. 151–168). Greenwich, CT: JAI Press.

Graham, P. S. (1995, July). Requirements for the digital research library. *College & Research Libraries, 56,* 331–339.

Hatcher, K. A. (1995). The role of the systems librarian/administrator: A report of the survey. *Library Administration & Management, 9,* 106–109.

Hawks, C. P. (1988, June). Management information gleaned from automated library systems. *Information Technology and Libraries, 7,* 131–138.

Hoffmann, E. (1991). Staff training issues in management of information services. In A. H. Helal, & J. W. Weiss (Eds.), *Information technology and library management.* 13th International Essen Symposium, 22–25 October 1990, Universitatsbibliothek Essen.

Huston, M. M., & Grahn, A. (1991). Management strategies for enhancing the adoption of technological innovations. In A. H. Helal & J. W. Weiss (Eds.), *Information technology and library management.* 13th International Essen Symposium, 22–25 October 1990, Universitatsbibliothek Essen.

Imhoff, K. (1996). *Making the most of new technology: A how-to-do-it manual for librarians.* New York: Neal-Schuman.

Jafari, A. (2003). The ABCs of designing campus portals. In A. Jafari & M. Sheehan (Eds.), *Designing portals: Opportunities and challenges* (pp. 7–27). Hershey, PA: Information Science.

Jones, H. D. (1956). A Librarian's View. In: *Recruiting Library Personnel/ Automation in the Library. Report of the 41st Conference of Eastern College Librarians* (pp. 40–43). Chicago: Association of College and Reference Libraries.

Jones, P. J. (2002, September). Rethinking library development. *C&RL News, 63,* 584–585.

Kalin, S. W. (1991, winter). Support services for remote users of online public access catalogs. *RQ, 31,* 197–213.

Kohl, D. F. (1995). Revealing UnCover. *Online, 19,* 52–60.

Kriz, H. M., & Queijo, Z. K. (1989). An environmental approach to library staff training. In S. Glogoff (Ed.), *Staff training in the automated library environment: A symposium. Library Hi Tech, 7,* 62–66.

Lakos, A., & Gray, C. (2000). Personalized library portals as an organizational culture change agent. *Information Technology and Libraries, 19,* 169–174.

Lancaster, F. W., & Sandore, B. (1997). *Technology and management in library and information services.* Champaign: University of Illinois GSLIS.

Laurence, H. (1997, March/April). Technological transformations: The evolution of a systems librarian. *Florida Libraries, 40,* 62–63.

Lavagnino, M. B. (1997, May). Networking and the role of the academic systems librarian: An evolutionary perspective. *College & Research Libraries, 58,* 217–231.

Lavagnino, M. B. (1998, fall). And on the eighth day: Creating a library systems office in the late 90s. *Library Administration & Management, 12,* 213–219.

Leonard, B. G. (1993, spring). The role of the systems librarian/administrator: A preliminary report. *Library Administration & Management, 7,* 113–116.

Leung, S., & Bisom, D. (Compilers). (1996). *Information technology policies* (SPEC kit 218). Washington, DC: Association of Research Libraries, Office of Management Studies.

Low, K. (1999). *Recruiting library staff: A how-to-do-it manual for librarians.* New York: Neal-Schuman.

Lugg, R., & Fischer R. *The Real Cost of ILS Ownership.* R2 Consulting Services, 2003 [white paper].

Luker M., & Peterson R. (Eds.). (2003). *Computer and network security in higher education* (EDUCAUSE Leadership Strategies No. 8). San Francisco: Jossey-Bass.

Machovec, G. S. (1991). The technology of change: What's involved and how it is accomplished. In G. M. Pitkin (Ed.), *Library systems migration: Changing automated systems in libraries and information centers.* Westport, CT: Meckler.

Martin, S. K. (1988). The role of the systems librarian. *Journal of Library Administration, 9,* 57–68.

McDonald, D. R. (1991). The management of information technology in libraries. In A. H. Helal & J. W. Weiss (Eds.), *Information technology and library management.* 13th International Essen Symposium, 22–25 October 1990: Universitatsbibliothek Essen.

Michael, J. J., & Hinnebusch, M. (1995). *From A to Z39.50.* Westport, CT: Mecklermedia.

Miller, W. (Ed.). (1989). Developing managerial competence for library automation. *Library Hi Tech, 7,* 103–112.

Morris, A., & Dyer, H. (1998). *Human aspects of library automation.* Brookfield, VT: Gower.

Muir, S. P. (Compiler). (1995). *Library systems office organization* (SPEC kit 211). Washington, DC: Association of Research Libraries, Office of Management Studies.

Muir, S. P., & Lim, A. (Compilers). (2002). *Library systems office organization* (SPEC kit 271). Washington, DC: Association of Research Libraries, Office of Management Studies.

Muirhead, G. (1994). Systems librarians in the UK: The results of a survey. In G. Muirhead (Ed.), *The systems librarian: The role of the library systems manager.* London: Library Association.

Myllis, H. (1990). Information systems planning as a tool of developing work: The case of statistics library. *INSPEL, 21,* 28–36.

Negroponte, N. (1995). *Being digital.* New York: Knopf.

Nielsen, B. (1989). Comments on developing managerial competence for library automation. In W. Miller (Ed.), Developing managerial competence for library automation. *Library Hi Tech, 7,* 103–112.

Ogg, H. (1997.) *Introduction to the use of computers in libraries: A textbook for the non-technical student.* Medford, NJ: Information Today.

Parkhurst, C. A. (1990, March/April). The in-house expert: The role of the systems librarian. *Library Software Review, 9,* 96–97.

Peters, P. E. (1988, June). A framework for the development of performance measurement standards. *Information Technology and Libraries, 7,* 193–197.

Piternick, G. (1970). The machine and cataloging. *Advances in Librarianship, 1,* 1–35.

Pitkin, G. M. (Ed.). 1991. *Library systems migration: Changing automated systems in libraries and information centers.* Westport, CT: Meckler.

Quinlan, C. A. (1991). The paradox of change: From turnkey system to in-house design. In G. M. Pitkin (Ed.), *Library systems migration* (pp. 86–101). Westport, CT: Meckler.

Rockman, I. (2003). Fun in the workplace. *Reference Services Review, 31,* 213–219.

Ronan, J., & Turner, C. (Compilers). (2002). *Chat Reference* (SPEC kit 273). Washington, DC: Association of Research Libraries, Office of Management Studies.

Ross, C., & Dewdney, P. (1998). *Communicating professionally: A how-to-do-it manual for librarians* (2nd ed.). New York: Neal-Schuman.

Sapp, G., & Gilmour, R. (2002). A brief history of the future of academic libraries: Predictions and speculations from the literature of the profession, 1975 to 2000—part one, 1975 to 1989. *Portal: Libraries and the Academy, 2,* 553–576.

Schwartz, C. A. (1997). *Restructuring academic libraries: Organizational development in the wake of technological change.* Chicago: Association of College and Research Libraries.

Sherman, C., & Price, G. (2001). *The invisible Web: Uncovering information sources search engines can't see.* Medford, NJ: Information Today.

Swan, J. (2002). *Fundraising for libraries: 25 proven ways to get more money for your library.* New York: Neal-Schuman.

Sweeney, R. T. (1994, summer). Leadership in the post-hierarchical library. *Library Trends, 43,* 62–94.

Tennant, R. (1998, February 15). The most important management decision: Hiring staff for the new millennium. *Library Journal, 123,*102.

Tennant, R. (Ed.). (2002). *XML in libraries.* New York: Neal-Schuman.

Trotta, M. (1995). *Successful staff development: A how-to-do-it manual for librarians.* New York: Neal-Schuman.

Turkle, S. (1991). If the computer is a tool, is it more like a hammer or more like a harpsichord? *National Forum, 71,* 8–11.

Waller, N. (2003, July/August). Model RFP for Integrated Library System Products. *Library Technology Reports, 39.*

Walster, D. (1993). *Managing time: A how-to-do-it manual for librarians.* New York: Neal-Schuman.

Walters, S. (1994). *Customer service: A how-to-do-it manual for librarians.* New York: Neal-Schuman.

Warner, A. S. (1998). *Budgeting: A how-to-do-it manual for librarians.* New York: Neal-Schuman.

Wasserman, P. (1965). *The librarian and the machine.* Detroit: Gale Research.

Weber, D. C. (1971, March). Personnel aspects of library automation. *Journal of Library Automation, 4,* 27–37.

White, F. (1990, August). The role of the automation librarian in the medium-sized library. *Canadian Library Journal, 47,* 257–259, 262.

Wilson, T. C. (1989). Training reference staff for automation in a transitional environment. In S. Glogoff (Ed.), Staff training in the automated library environment: A symposium [special issue]. *Library Hi Tech, 7,* 67–70.

Wilson, T. C. (1998). *The systems librarian: Designing roles and defining skills.* Chicago: American Library Association.

Woodward, Jeannette. (2000). *Countdown to a new library: Managing the building project.* Chicago: American Library Association.

Wright, K. C., & Davie, J. F. (1991). *Serving the disabled: A how-to-do-it manual for librarians.* New York: Neal-Schuman.

Additional Reading

Association of Research Libraries, Office of Management Studies. (1991). *Organization charts in ARL libraries* (SPEC kit 170). Compiled by J. M. Poole. Washington, DC: ARL.

Association of Research Libraries, Office of Management Studies. (1994). *User surveys in ARL Libraries* (SPEC kit 205). Compiled by E. Brekke. Washington, DC: ARL.

Association of Research Libraries, Office of Management Studies. (1999). *Web page development and management* (SPEC kit 246). Compiled by Y. P. Liu. Washington, DC: ARL.

Association of Research Libraries, Office of Management Studies. (2001). *Staffing the library web site* (SPEC kit 266). Compiled by K. Ragsdale. Washington, DC: ARL.

Burke, J. J. (2001). *Library Technology Companion: A Basic Guide for Library Staff*. New York: Neal-Schuman.

Carson, P. P., Carson, K. D., & Phillips, J. S. (1995). *Library manager's deskbook: 102 expert solutions to 101 common dilemmas*. Chicago: American Library Association.

Cohn, J. M., Kelsey, A. L., & Fiels, K. M. (1997). *Planning for automation* (2nd ed.). New York: Neal-Schuman.

Crawford, W. (1988). *Current technologies in the library*. Boston: G. K. Hall.

Drew, B. (2002, July 15). The wireless student & the library. *LJOnline*. http://www.libraryjournal.com/index.asp?layout=article&articleid=CA232340

Gardner, J. J. (1979). *Resource notebook on planning*. Washington, DC: ARL Office of Management Studies.

Helal, A. H., & Weiss, J. W. (Eds.). (1991). *Information technology and library management*. 13th International Essen Symposium, 22–25 October 1990, Universitatsbibliothek Essen.

Hewitt, J. A. (Ed.). (1987). *Advances in library automation and networking* (vol. 1). Greenwich, CT: JAI Press.

Hodges, M. S. (1999). *Computers: systems, terms and acronyms* (11th ed.). Winter Park, FL: SemCo Enterprises.

Lancaster, F.W. (1978). *Toward Paperless Information Systems.* New York: Academic Press.

Luce, R. E. (1989). Developing managerial competence in information technology. In W. Miller (Ed.), Developing managerial competence for library automation [special issue]. *Library Hi Tech, 7,* 103–112.

McInerney, C., Daley, A., & Vandergrift, K. E. (2002). Broadening our reach: LIS education for undergraduates. *American Libraries, 33,* 40–43.

Pfohl, D., & Hayes, S. (2001, November/December). Today's systems librarians have a lot to juggle. *Computers in Libraries,* 30–33.

Rieger, O.Y., & Kenney, A.R. (2000). *Moving theory into practice: Digital imaging for libraries and archives.* Mountain View, CA: Research Libraries Group.

Trzeciak, J. (2003). Special section on personal digital assistants (PDAs). *Library Hi Tech, 21,* 393–439.

Index

Academic libraries, xi–xiv, 23–25, 41, 44–45. *See also* Gorman, M.; Sapp, G.
Access points, 106. *See also* Wireless
Accreditation, 71, 176
ACM. *See* Association for Computing Machinery
Administration. *See* Library administration
ALA. *See* American Library Association
Allen, N., 4
American Library Association, 43, 45, 51
American National Standards Institute, 113, 176
American Society for Information Science & Technology, 51, 70
ANSI. *See* American National Standards Institute
Antivirus. *See* Virus
API. *See* Application programming interface
Application programming interface, 98, 176
Applications, 8, 14–16, 30, 78, 81, 86, 98, 150, 179. *See also* Software
Appropriate use, 56, 135
ARL. *See* Association of Research Libraries
Asbestos, 103, 105. *See also* Safety
ASIST. *See* American Society for Information Science & Technology
Assessment
    of personnel, 4–5, 36–37, 41, 44–45, 74, 159–63
    of technology, 14, 16, 64–65, 93, 109–12, 130
Association for Computing Machinery, 70

Association of Research Libraries, 4, 6, 8, 11–12, 27, 51–52, 88, 97, 180
Audience, 3, 42–43, 68–69, 88
Authentication, 94, 107, 125, 130. *See also* Passwords
Automation, xii, 26, 137. *See also* History of information technology in libraries

Backups, 91–92, 96, 118, 145–46. *See also* Security
Bandwidth, 83, 106, 129
Barber, D., 111
Barclay, D., 4, 85, 93, 104, 108, 112–13
Bid process, 19–20, 176. *See also* Migration; Request for information; Request for proposal; Request for quote; Cortez, E. M.; Waller, N.
Bishoff, L., 4
Bisom, D., 5
Blogs, 122–23, 176
Boss, R. W., 2, 13, 17, 90
Branch libraries, 24, 30–32. *See also* Decentralization
Branse, Y., 99
Breeding, M., 13, 17
Brown, J., 14
Browsers (Lynx, Mosaic, Netscape, Internet Explorer, Opera), 52, 86, 98, 129, 149. *See also* World Wide Web
Budget, 7, 18–19, 55–57, 68, 89. *See also* Planning; Project management
Buildings, Books and Bytes, 3–4, 8

Cabling, 105, 108
Campus computing, 2, 49, 69–70, 84, 90
CD-ROM, 84–85, 118

Centralization, 30–32
CGI. *See* Common Gateway Interface
Change, xii–xiv, 1, 3, 8, 14, 23, 28, 29, 34, 45–46, 109
Chat, 74, 123–25
Children's Internet Protection Act, 93
Chu, F. T., 10, 34
CIPA. *See* Children's Internet Protection Act
CLIR. *See* Council on Library and Information Resources (CLIR)
CNI. *See* Coalition for Networked Information
Coalition for Networked Information, 51, 70, 101
Collegiality, 41–42. *See also* Communication; Consensus
Colorado Alliance of Research Libraries, 50, 129
Common Gateway Interface, 98
Communication, 5, 39–48
Computer census, 79–80, 149–50
Computers, 18–19, 79–83, 108, 130. *See also* Automation
Configuration, 79–81, 178
Connell, T. H., 28, 39, 111, 113
Consensus, 5. *See also* Communication; Collegiality
Consortia, 50, 118
Consultants, 137
Continuing education, 73–75. *See also* Staff development
Contracts, 17, 19–20, 28, 50, 89. *See also* Bid process
Controlled circulation, xii, 154
Corbly, J. E., 18, 40, 86
Cortez, E. M., 17
Cost, 14, 19, 82, 85, 89, 92, 104
Cost effectiveness, 9, 59, 79, 81
Cost recovery, 84
Council on Library and Information Resources (CLIR), 119
Croneis, K. S., 27
Cronin, M. J., 13, 73
Current awareness, xii, 43–44, 154. See also Controlled circulation; Professional reading

Data protection, 80, 91–92, 96, 118, 145–46. *See also* Backups

Databases, 2, 15. *See also* Licensed databases
Davie, J. F., 109
De Klerk, A., 28–29, 36
Decentralization, 30–32
Decision making, 11–13, 29, 116, 155–56
Degree. *See* Master of Library Science (MLS)
Deployment, 79–81
Development (financial), 55–57
Dewdney, P., 41
DHCP. *See* Dynamic host configuration protocol (DHCP)
Dictionaries, 176
Digital divide, 65, 128
Digital versatile disk (DVD), 84–85, 118
Digitization, xi, 5, 116–20, 128–29. *See also* Barber, D.
Disaster, 20–21, 92, 138–48
Discussion groups. *See* Listservs
Distance learning, 98, 124–25, 130
Distributed resources, 30
DNS. *See* Domain name service
Document delivery, 125–26
Documentation, 10, 14–15, 20, 71, 91, 95–96, 104–105
Domain name service (DNS), 83, 176
Dougherty, R. M., 71–73
Downloading, 84, 134
Drivers, 86–87
Dublin Core. *See* Metadata
Dunsire, G., 26, 78
DVD. *See* Digital versatile disk (DVD)
Dvorak, J. C., 19
Dyer, H., 46, 107–108
Dynamic host configuration protocol (DHCP), 80, 83, 104, 176

E-mail, 39, 42–43, 50, 61, 63–65, 84, 91, 93, 121, 124, 126, 135–36
EAD. *See* Metadata
Education, 67–75
Educational Resources Information Center, 45, 176
Elliot, V., 99
Email. *See* E-mail
Emergencies, 20–21, 92, 138–48

Encoded archival description. *See* Metadata

Epstein, S. B., 35

Equipment, 18–20, 79–83, 85, 108, 117, 130, 151–53

Ergonomics, 107–108

ERIC. *See* Educational Resources Information Center

Ethernet, 105–106. *See also* Cabling

Euster, J. R., 28–29, 36

Eustis, J. D., 4, 29

Evaluation
    of personnel, 4–5, 36–37, 41, 44–45, 74, 159–63
    of technology, 14, 16, 64–65, 93, 109–12, 130

Executive summary, 13

Extensible markup language, 51, 114, 122

Facilities, 101–107. *See also* Space

FAQs. *See* Frequently asked questions

Federated searching, 129

Fees, 5–6, 56–57, 84

File transfer protocol, 176

Filtering, 85

Firewalls, 94, 107, 125

Fischer, R., 14

Foote, M., 26–27, 39, 49, 67, 71

Franklin, C., 28, 39, 111, 113

Freeman, G., 35

Frequently asked questions (FAQs), 43, 62, 176

FTP. *See* File transfer protocol

Full text, 44, 52, 83–84, 116, 125, 129

Funding, 5–6, 18, 56–57, 84, 151

Furniture, 9, 107–108

Gateway, 83. *See also* Common Gateway Interface

Gilbert, S. W., 111

Gilmour, R., xii, xiv

Glogoff, S., 73

Gold Rush, 129

Gordon, B., 98

Gordon, R. S., xiii, 71

Gorman, M., xiv, 5, 25, 28, 56, 60–61, 109, 118

Graham, P. S., 6, 52, 55

Grahn, A., 8, 40

Grants, 57. *See also* Swan, J.

Gray, C., 116

Hardware. *See* Computers; Networks; Servers; Space

Hatcher, K. A., 2, 50

Hawks, C. P., 12

Heating, ventilation, and air-conditioning (HVAC), 102, 104

HEGIS. *See* Higher Education General Information Survey

Help desk, 43, 60–64

Henderson, P., 27

Hierarchy, 28–31

Higher education, 4, 11, 44, 67, 70, 93, 98, 111, 123, 128, 130–31

Higher Education General Information Survey (HEGIS), 11

Hinnebusch, M., 17, 105

Hiring. *See* Recruiting

History of information technology in libraries, xii–xiv. *See also* Gorman, M.; Wilson, T. C.; Sapp, G.

Hodges, M. S., 176

Hoffmann, E., 39, 68, 74

Humor, 45, 47

Huston, M. M., 8, 40

HVAC. *See* Heating, ventilation, and air conditioning

IEEE. *See* Institute of Electrical and Electronic Engineers

ILS. *See* Integrated Library Systems

Imaging. *See* Digitization

Imhoff, K., 10, 18, 50

Information technology, 2, 6, 10, 35, 40–41, 65–66, 68, 72, 79–80, 83, 93, 164–72

Infrastructure, 103–106

Institute of Electrical and Electronic Engineers (IEEE), 106, 114, 176

Institutional repositories, 130

Integrated Library Systems, 13–17, 26, 50–51, 69, 97, 110, 126, 157, 176

Integrated Postsecondary Education Data System. *See* Higher Education General Information Survey

Integration, 9, 51, 117, 128
Intellectual freedom, 6
Intellectual ownership, 6
Interactive chat. *See* Chat
International standards, 112–15
International Standards Organization
    (ISO), 78, 114
Internet, xiii–xiv, 1, 4, 24, 44, 69, 72,
    85, 93, 105, 107, 110–11,
    114–15, 128–29, 134
Internet2, 130, 167
Intranet, 5, 39, 65, 74, 125
Inventory, 96–97, 103
IPEDS. *See* Higher Education General
    Information Survey
IRC. *See* Chat
ISO. *See* International Standards
    Organization (ISO)
IT. *See* Information technology

Jafari, A., 115
Java, 98. *See also* Programming
Job descriptions, 28, 36–37, 41, 158
Jones, H.D., xii
Jones, P. J., 55–56

Kalin, S. W., 60–61, 110
Kenney, D. J., 4, 29
Kohl, D. F., 43
Kriz, H. M., xiii, 73–74

LAN. *See* Local area networks
Lakos, A., 116
Laptop computers, 33, 106, 120, 122,
    170–71. *See also* Mobile
    computing
Lancaster, F. W., xii, 12, 28, 52, 110
Laurence, H., xiii
Lavagnino, M. B., xiii–xiv, 7, 25, 27,
    40, 59, 65
Leadership, 26, 41, 45–46
Learning. *See* Continuing education;
    Education; Training
Leonard, B. G., 10
Leung, S., 5
Liability, 107, 122
LibQUAL, 8
Library & Information Technology
    Association (LITA), 65, 70, 116

Library administration, xiv, 23, 28,
    31–32, 35, 40, 55, 105, 153,
    155–56
Library of Congress, xii, 18
Licensed databases, 56, 81, 87–88, 90
Link checking, 99
Listservs, 39, 70, 108, 180–81
LITA. *See* Library & Information
    Technology Association
Local area networks, 18, 26, 105–106,
    134–35
Local standards, 17–18
Logs, 25, 43, 69, 74, 96. *See also* Blogs
Low, K., 36
Lugg, R., 14
Luker, M., 93

Machine readable cataloging (MARC),
    xii, 17–18, 99, 113–14, 117
Machovec, G. S., 14, 16, 114
Maintenance, 81–85
Management data. *See* Statistics
Management style. *See* Collegiality;
    Evaluation of personnel
MARC. *See* Machine readable
    cataloging (MARC)
Marketing, 16, 42, 56, 60, 65, 123, 127
Martin, S. K., xiii, 27
Master of Library Science (MLS),
    71–72
McDonald, D. R., 5
Mentoring, 128
Metadata, 2, 114, 117–18, 129, 165–66
Michael, J. J., 17, 105
Migration, 13–17, 85. *See also* Pitkin,
    G. M.
Miller, W., 34, 71, 74
Mission critical, 103, 111–12
Mission of the library, 5, 42
MLS. *See* Master of Library Science
Mobile computing, 107, 120–22. *See*
    also Laptops
Monitoring, 86–88, 90–91, 94
Morris, A., 46, 107–108
Muir, S. P., 7, 23, 24
Muirhead, G., 23, 39, 46, 71
Multimedia, 111. *See also* CD-ROM;
    Digital versatile disk (DVD)
Myllis, H., 7, 46

National Information Standards
    Organization, 113–14
National organizations, 50–51
Negroponte, N., 16, 128
Networks, *See* Internet; Intranet; Local
    area networks
New technology, 128–30. *See also*
    Current awareness; Professional
    reading
Newsgroups, 93
Nielsen, B., 73–74, 109
NISO. *See* National Information
    Standards Organization

Ogg, H., 77
Open source, 64, 98, 115
OpenURL, 113–14, 128–29. *See also*
    Federated searching
Operating system. *See* Platforms
Operations, 77–99
Organization charts, xiv, 28–33
Organizational change. *See* Change
OSI model, 77–78
Outsourcing, 8, 52, 75, 102, 117, 166

Parkhurst, C. A., 7, 39
Partnerships, 57
Passwords, 62, 90, 94, 115, 134–35,
    174. *See also* Security
Patches. *See* Software
Patrons. *See* Audience
PDA. *See* Personal digital assistant
Performance review. *See* Evaluation of
    personnel
PERL. *See* Practical extraction and
    report language
Personal digital assistant, 106, 120–22,
    129
Personnel. *See* Recruiting; Evaluation of
    personnel
PERT. *See* Program evaluation and
    review technique
Peters, P. E., 14
Peterson, R., 93
Phones. *See* Telephones
Pin, L., 99
Piternick, G., xii
Pitkin, G. M., 17
Planning tools, 7–9
Platforms, 14–15, 89, 121

Policy, 4–6, 134–35, 174, 179
Politics, 5, 128
Portals, 6, 115–16
PR. *See* Public relations
Practical extraction and report language
    (PERL), 34, 64, 98. *See also*
    Programming
Price, G., 44
Printing, 2, 79, 83–84, 86, 95, 168, 170
Privacy, 91. *See also* Passwords; Virtual
    private network
Professional organizations, 70. *See also*
    National organizations
Professional reading, 75, 175. *See also*
    Current awareness
Program evaluation and review
    technique, 7, 177
Programming, 14, 35, 98–99
Project management, 10–11
Promotion and tenure, 44. *See also*
    Academic libraries
Prototyping, 79–81
Public relations (PR), 5, 56, 123
Publication (academic), 5, 41, 44. *See
    also* Scholarship
Purchasing, 19–20, 50, 53

Queijo, Z. K., xiii, 73–74
Quinlan, C. A., 1, 3

Radio frequency identification, 120
Record keeping, 85, 91, 96
Recruiting, 34–36, 44, 74, 155
Recycling, 81. *See also* Reselling
Remote users, 6, 9, 33–34, 42–43,
    60–61, 64, 83, 87–88, 91, 113,
    124–25. *See also* Kalin, S. W.
Removable storage, 85. *See also*
    CD-ROM; Digital versatile disk
    (DVD)
Replacement, 18–19, 151
Reports
    Decision making 2, 11–16, 97–98
    Problem. *See* Help desk
Request for information, 17
Request for proposal, 17, 113. *See also*
    Waller, N.
Request for quote, 17. *See also* Bid
    process

Research
Professional, 4, 6–8, 12, 41, 43–45
Technical, 2, 62, 92, 102, 109–11, 164
Reselling, 81
Resource sharing. *See* Consortia
Restricting access, 88, 93, 124–25. *See also* Filtering; Licensed databases; Passwords
Retention of employees, 25, 67. *See also* Training
Reviews. *See* Evaluation: of personnel
RFI. *See* Request for information
RFID. *See* Radio frequency identification
RFP. *See* Request for proposal
RFQ. *See* Request for quote
Rockman, I., 47
Ronan, J., 124
Ross, C., 41
Rotation. *See* Replacement
Routing, 43, 63, 175. *See also* Current awareness

Safety, 105–108. *See also* Asbestos; Ergonomics
Salaries, 12, 27, 166
SAN. *See* Storage: Network
Sandore, B., 12, 28, 52, 110
Sapp. G., xii, xiv
Scholarship, 44. *See also* Research: Professional; Publication
Schwartz, C. A., 28
Scripting, 98. *See also* Programming
SDI. *See* Selective dissemination of information
Security, 92–94, 107. *See also* Monitoring; Passwords
Selective dissemination of information, 43
Server utilities. *See* Monitoring
Servers, xii, 15, 20, 69, 78–79, 82, 84, 87, 89–92, 94, 178
Service, 59–66
Sherman, C., 44
Shibboleth, 130
Skills. *See* Training
Software, 8, 14–16, 30, 78, 81, 86, 98, 150, 179. *See also* Applications
Space, 30, 101–107. *See also* Facilities

Specifications, 82
Staff development, 73–75, 109. *See also* Continuing education; Training
Staffing, 81, 82, 85, 89, 95, 98–99, 103, 117, 155. *See also* Hierarchy; Recruitment; Teams
Stakeholders, 5, 49, 15, 18, 25, 29, 45–46, 49, 156
Standards, 106, 113. *See also* International standards; Local standards; Service
Statistics, 2, 9, 11–13, 16, 97–98
Storage
Physical, 30, 101
Network, 80, 118. *See also* CD-ROM; Digital versatile disk (DVD); Removable storage
Strategic planning, 3–4. *See also* Technology plan
Streaming, 117
Stress, 46–47.
Support
for staff, 33–34, 59–66, 116–17, 119, 126, 130, 168, 179. See also Help desk; Telecommuting
for the public, 42–43, 59–66, 121, 168, 179. *See also* Help desk; Remote users
Swan, J., 57
Sweeney, R. T., 28, 33, 45, 79, 109, 111

Teaching, 12, 42, 67–68, 98, 111, 120, 125, 127, 168, 181. *See also* Continuing education; Education; Higher education; Staff development; Training
Teams, 24, 28–30, 155–56
Technology fees, 6, 56–57
Technology plan, 2, 10, 64, 164–72. *See also* Strategic planning
Telecommuting, 33–34
Telephones, 14, 43, 61, 63–64, 102, 105–106
Tennant, R., 34, 114
Testing (equipment), 14, 29, 79–81, 93, 113, 116, 121
Thin clients, 129
Total Quality Management, 7
TQM. *See* Total Quality Management

Training, xii, 9, 15, 30, 34–35, 39–40, 44, 46, 61–63, 67–75, 87, 89, 90, 95–97, 106, 110, 119–20, 124–25, 127. *See also* Continuing education; Staff development; Teaching
Trends
in Higher education, 130–31
in Technology, 128–30
Trotta, M., 37, 46, 74
Turkle, S., 115
Turner, C., 124

Uniform resource locator. *See* Universal resource locator
Universal resource locator, 16, 99, 129, 180–81. *See also* OpenURL
Upgrades, 81, 86–87
URL. *See* Universal resource locator
Usenet. *See* Newsgroups
User groups, 51, 60, 70, 89
Users. *See* Audience

Vendors, 12, 51–53, 64, 70, 84, 88–89, 93–94, 124, 157
Videoconferencing, 123

Virtual private network, 94, 107
Viruses, 86, 90, 93–94, 180
VPN. *See* Virtual private network

Waller, N., 17
Walster, D., 11, 45, 47, 101
Walters, S., 60
Warner, A. S., 7
Wasserman, P., xii–xiii
Web logs. *See* Blogs
Weber, D. C., 35
White, F., 3, 12, 46, 68, 95
Wiki, 124–25
Wilson, T. C., xiii–xiv, 9, 28, 69, 71, 73–74
Wireless, 94, 105–107, 114, 120–22, 129, 170–71, 181. *See also* Access points; Ethernet; Local area networks; Mobile computing
Woodward, J., 104
World Wide Web (WWW), xiii, 16, 69, 98, 111, 134
Worm. *See* Virus
Wright, K. C., 108

XML. *See* Extensible markup language

About the Authors

Pat Ingersoll is the Associate Director for Library Systems and Associate Professor at the University of Denver, Penrose Library. She has spent more than twenty years working in academic libraries. Her other research interests include staff development and resource sharing.

John Culshaw is Associate Professor and Faculty Director for Systems at the University of Colorado at Boulder Libraries. He has worked in academic libraries for more than fifteen years. He has also served the academic library community as chair of the international Innovative Users Group and facilitator of the Rocky Mountain Regional Innovative Users Group.